The Journey Begins

By

Catherine Mae Clifford

Table of Contents

Acknowledgements

I praise and thank the Lord our God for His incred-ible faithfulness, love, grace, mercy and long suffering. Every step I have ever taken was truly ordered and ordained by Him! Through the writing of this book, He proved that to me in exciting and fresh ways. May His name be praised forever! Every word, every experience, every parable was given to me by our Lord God—I take credit for nothing but being a tube that He choose to flow through. Who are we that He would ever consider us, let alone choose to use us for His beautiful glory! Keep your eyes fixed on Him.

For my husband and the understanding and long-suffering he had for me while God was bringing me through healing and dealing with the "stuff" in my own heart! I am so glad that God brought you to me! Thanks for your love and understanding!

Introduction

No matter if you are seeking to find healing for your soul or just desire to be encouraged, I believe that these stories will help you find what your heart desires. As you read these little stories, understand that they are the heart of God for you. He has plans for you—to prosper you and not to harm you, to give you a hope and a future. (Jeremiah 29:11 NIV) He alone is God, and there are no accidents in Him. Therefore, if this has fallen into your hands understand that He desires to speak to you as you walk with my family and me on these beautiful hikes. My prayer is that you would realize that God is the God of all hope and that no matter what happens to you, He is well able to keep you through all the trials, tribulations, sicknesses, losses, heartaches and joys in your life! Just keep your eyes focused on HIM!!! When you focus on Him, you will be amazed that all else will completely dim in your life—and as you raise Him up, all the enemies of your life will become so small, completely under your feet! They overcame him by the blood of the Lamb and the word of their testimony; they did not love their lives so much as to shrink from death. (Revelation 12:11 NIV)

For those of you who do not have a relationship with the Lord of all, I pray that this book will give you such a hunger and thirst for Him and His glorious presence that you will seek Him until He is found by you! He is no respecter of persons. What He has done for me He is well able to do for you! He loves you so much that He stretched out His arms and feet on a cross and died for you. Now He stands with open arms, knocking on the door of your heart, waiting for you to welcome Him in! It is up to you, just let Him in, then you will have life and that life more abundantly—and the devil will no longer be able to steal, kill or destroy! (See John 10:10) You see, at that point when you ask the Lord Jesus in your heart, you will belong to Him!

Blessings be upon you! My prayer is that you would feel His presence around you as you read this little epistle of His great love, mercy and grace on a sinner such as me! And now, let the journey begin!

But those who suffer
he delivers in their suffering;
He speaks to them in their affliction.
"He is wooing you from the
jaws of distress
to a spacious place
free from restriction,
to the comfort
of your table
laden with choice food.
Job 36:15-16

The Beginning

Chapter 1

My husband loves the mountains—so hiking was one of the activities that our family enjoyed. I remember the beginnings of the journey to the top of the mountains! Everyone is so excited, and we could not wait to see the sights and landscape that would be on the trip to the top. As we would begin, we wondered what wildlife we would encounter, what flowers would we see, would there be rivers and falls along the way and how difficult would the trail be? We had our cameras right by our sides ready to take pictures of the incredible sights.

Each mountain had a quest to conquer. Some were waterfalls, some were the view, some were caves—but all the mountains had a quest or a goal. Many times we began those hikes not really under-standing all we would have to encounter— how much perseverance it would take, the right equipment that was needed and making sure we had enough water and food to make it. Some hikes were quite pleasant, and others quite grueling. Each one I remember and with each one a new lesson was learned. You see, you cannot live on top of the mountain—that is not where life takes place, it is in the valleys and on the trip up that life is experienced. The same is true with our Christian journey—the mountaintops are incredible—the views are spectacular and awesome. Each time we get to the top of a mountain, we get to see our Lord in a whole new light. Wow! How I love those mountaintops! But life is not what happens on top of the mountain, it is what happens on the journey up and the return trip down. The tops of the mountains are only a resting place for the trip down.

There is much to be learned in the valley and on the trip up and down. It is where the rubber meets the road, where we actually see what is inside our hearts. Where we see how much we have paid attention to the love letters our Lord has given us. It is where the good, bad and ugly come out of us and it is where character is developed and shaped!

Also in the valley is where flowers bloom, the birds sing, disappointments are faced and true life happens. On the journey up, is where our perseverance and patience are tested not only with ourselves, but with those on the journey with us. So much will be learned about ourselves on these journeys. The amazing thing is that God is faithful and will not allow us to be tempted beyond that which we can bear and with that temptation, He will make a way of escape so that we will be able to bear up under it.

He also places people around to encourage us when we get weary in doing good—and start to lose hope. When we keep our focus, realizing that He is also with us through the trip, then we will understand nothing will harm us. After all, He is interested in our character not our comfort!

Here we are, just beginning this journey. Where will it go, what will it be like, what will we see, can we do this, can we trust Him? All these questions are going through our minds—yet at the same time; we know He loves us, just look at the cross. Should that not tell us He does have our best in mind? In His love letter to us, He said, "For I know the plans I have for you declares the Lord, plans to prosper you and not to harm you, to give you a hope and a future." (Jeremiah 29:11) He knows where we need to go and what needs to happen in our lives in order for us to fulfill the purpose and plan He has for us in life. He sees the big picture; we are only a pea in the valley—so let us learn to completely trust Him.

Here goes—our first step on this journey, facing our self for who we really are. In order for us to truly have this new life and begin this journey, there will come a time that we must come face to face with who we really are. You see no matter what we have gone through, we alone made the choices to be who we have become. No matter how much our parents may or may not have failed to be who we needed them to be, no matter how violent or brutal life has been to us, or how easy we have had it, we are responsible for who we have chosen to become. There is no perfect life—no fairy tale story with a happily ever after ending—we all have sinned and fallen short of the glory of God! (Romans 3:23) Once we begin to come to this realization we find ourselves looking honestly at who we have become in God's spiritual mirror. This is lovingly called coming to the end of ourselves. Only then can we begin to see what is really there, in our hearts. You know what I mean. Who we are without all the makeup, grooming, the right clothes, the right speech, or being part of the "right" crowd, the correct manners—just "appearing" like we have it all together on the outside. If only they could see the inside! So many times we even convinced ourselves we are OK—it was "them" they were a mess and needed help— not us. After all, we are successful and doing great now. But deep inside our heart we know we are full of anger, bitterness, pride, arrogance, and unforgivness—even anger at God! We never thought about the fact that it was us who chose to embrace anger, unforgivness, pride, arrogance and bitterness instead of trying to understand and choose love, humility, meekness, forgiveness, and compassion. But through the whole time, God has seen right through all the fluff and still loves us and still chooses to work with us. He has not given up on us—so do not give up on yourself or others.

We cannot compare ourselves to any other person in this mirror; we compare ourselves to Jesus Himself. We cannot look at another soul and say, "Well I'm better than they are—after all, I give to the poor, I help the needy, and even bring people food and take them to the doctor as they need. I am a good person full or good works and successful in my career." I have to ask—good by whose standards, yours or God's? When you look into this mirror, you are looking into the eyes of Love Himself! You see, He sees past the mistakes, the heartaches, the failures and tears and sees your heart! Only He knows what is in your heart! Scripture tells us, the heart is deceitful and deceitful above all things and beyond cure. Who can understand it? (Jer17:9) This means that we do not even know our own hearts! So many times in my journey with the Lord, He brought up something that was there that shocked me realizing this was in my heart! But ugly as it was, there it was right in front of my face and it needed to be dealt with! Do not be afraid to see in the mirror—you are only looking at the beginning. He makes all things beautiful in its time! (Ecc 3:11a). Your whole job from this point on is to allow Him to make you into this beautiful person He desires you to be.

When the Lord brought me to this point I remember hesitating. The Lord asked me, "What are you afraid of Child?" I thought for a second, and answered what I did not even realize I felt. But it was truth! I told the Lord, "What if Lord, I find out that all those things they said about me are true. Then how could I live?" Very sweetly our Lord spoke to me and said, "Child, that is what life made you to be, but what you are about to find out is who I am creating you to be. My Word promises you that I make ALL things beautiful in their time—that includes you!"

Friend, do not let fear stop you from allowing God to dig up the things that are holding you in bondage. You see, we will have a potter, something that molds and makes us. The key is which potter will we choose? As for me and my house we will serve the Lord! He is our potter. Remember we are the clay, he alone is the potter. The clay's only job is to sit in the center of the wheel and submit to the pressure of the potter's hand—the potter does the rest. He may cut away a few things, but you will find in the end that you did not need them after all. As you know after a potter finishes molding a vessel to his desire—the next step is placing it in the fire. Just like the hike, it is in the fire that the vessel is tested—and hardened in order to be fit for use! The wonderful thing is that we may go through the fire, but we will not be burned.

Isaiah 43 says we will go through the fire and not be burned— the flames will not set us ablaze—it will just burn off the thing that had us bound in the first place. Ultimately the goal for your life in God is that He would create you to be a beautiful vessel that He can put on display for the world to see that He truly does exist! Romans 8:28-29 says that "He works all things for the good of those who love Him and are called according to His purpose. For those He foreknew He also predestined to be conformed into the image of His Son Jesus Christ!" Dear friend, He is only conforming you—relax, enjoy the trip—do not forget to smell every flower, see every bird, enjoy the beautiful scenery and the rivers then realize that the same God that is taking you through is the same God that created all you are experiencing! WOW! What a mighty God we do serve! Is He not worthy of all our trust? Now let us begin the journey together!

The Marriage

Chapter 2

*Wait on the Lord, be strong and take heart
and wait for the Lord! (Psalm 27:14)*

Once my ex-husband walked out a healing
process began. God had a plan, in spite of
all my failures, wounds and heartaches. If there is
one thing I would love to get across to you, it is the
fact that our failures, the circumstances of life, the
disappointments, hurts and wounds others inflict on
us and those we inflict on ourselves, has little to do
with the plan God has for us! He amazingly uses all
that happens in life for His glory and for our good!
After all, isn't that what life is all about? Almost two
years after my ex-husband walked out the first time,
I was convinced that I had no need of a man in my
life again! After all, who in the world could compete
with Jesus? He was my all in all! He was there when

I went to sleep, there when I woke in the morning and wherever I was, He was there! He was my knight in shining armor, the song in my nights, a bright and morning star—He was the very breath I breathe! No way could any man come into my life and compete with my Lord! I was convinced that a man would only cramp my time with the Lord. My children and I were so happy and content—life was wonderful!

Whenever my Christian mom talked to me about meeting some man, I would promptly say—Men =sin or I would make a sign of the cross at her! It always gave me great joy because it really upset her! She would remind me that God had instituted marriage it was a God idea! I did not want anything to do with that institution! I had tried it before and was convinced that I was better off! After all, Paul tells us in Corinthians that those who marry WILL have trouble! I wanted no part of that "trouble"! I had had enough in life—I wanted to just bask in how awesome my God was and the fact that HE loved ME!!! Wow, ME, the God of all loved me!

HALT—wait a minute! Do you realize that contentment is wonderful, but we do not grow in contentment! It is proven that it is only through adversity that we grow; because, you see, through adversity we have to "prove" that we stand on the truth of the word of God! In other words, it is there in adversity we learn if we really believe what we say—it's where we get to walk it out! This was the children of Israel's problem in the wilderness and desert! They did not want any trouble—trials or testing! They wanted to have everything easy, handed to them. The sad thing is God was not able to do anything through these because of their unbelief in who HE was! That is the bottom line—do we believe Him or not?

Well, how was God going to do this? He is pretty sneaky sometimes and He does have a great sense of humor! He had a plan! By the way, He always has a plan! If you try to mess up His plan A, He does have a plan B that will end in the same result! His ways WILL succeed one way or another! Everywhere I went I met children from divorced homes. I drove many to the bus stop and sometimes to school; they were in church and in our neighborhood, even in my own home. They would open up and tell me how much it grieved them that sometimes their parents made them choose between each other, many did not see the parent that left and it caused such wounds in these children. I began to see just how desperately these kids needed someone they could count on to talk to that would give them godly advice and love them right where they were. That is when the "ministry plan" hit me, but little did I realize that God had an entirely different plan for this "ministry".

I went to my pastor and told him about it and we discussed creating a big brother, big sister program for kids from divorce. It would also be one way to reach out to the community if we could get enough volunteers. Immediately I started praying about it and getting excited! Wow, what God could do through this plan! Wow, the possibilities were unlimited! In my delusion of grander I could see whole families getting saved! Boy, what a great thing for the Kingdom of God! I had the whole thing figured out—I would just be the one who advertised and hooked up the big brothers and big sisters with the kids! Notice just how many times I said "I." I had my plans, but God had His own plan, and might I add, He was really sneaky at it! Oh how I love my Lord!

My neighbor and I were best friends and prayer partners and when I told her about the "plan"—the first thing she said was, "There's a guy at our church who has a daughter who could really use this." I said, "Tell him about it. And if he is interested, give him my phone number and I'll set her up with a big sister." You see, one of those "n" words that I had been saying was I will _n_ever call a man. I found out something very important! Do not EVER, NEVER tell God the "n" word—you know, never, no, not me!

Little did I realize that God was up to something entirely different than what I had planned. As I was praying about who would be this child's big sister, the Lord spoke to me and said, "You do it!"

I said, "What Lord?"

He said it again—"You do it!"

"But, Lord, that is not how I planned it! I was going to setup the big sisters and brothers—I did not want to be one!" After all, I do not have time and I'm a single parent—money is a tight!" Do you know something, God does not reason with you—He said it again!

"Daughter, YOU DO IT!"

Then He gave me a vision of this dear child sitting by a window crying out to Him for a mother!

It broke my heart because in a way I knew what she was feeling.

"Ok, Lord, but I just do not know how this is going to work!" Then my neighbor came over and gave me a card and said, that friend of mine wants you to call him! That was it! Not only did God want me to be a big sister, but now I had to call this guy! Was he crazy? Did he want help for his daughter or not? As you can see, I had a problem! My problem was called pride! God in His amazing wisdom was about to get started on the process of working all that out of my system! Little did I know what was next!

It was hours that I held that card in my hand just dumb founded over this whole situation—this was not turning out the way I had planned! There is a scripture that I dearly love in Isaiah 55:8-9:

> For my thoughts are not your thoughts, neither
> are your ways my ways, declares the Lord.
> As the heavens are higher than the earth so
> are my ways higher than your ways and my
> thoughts than your thoughts.

Have you ever lain down on the ground and looked up—there is a far piece from the ground to the sky, and to think that that is not the end! There is a whole universe out there still pass the blue sky! That is how different our thoughts are to His! We are peas in a valley, and He is God of all looking down on us! He sees the "big picture." We see a blade of grass! He is God! We are not!

Well, I finally picked up the phone to call this MAN! Right before he answered, I heard the Lord say, "Child, behold your new husband!"

As you could imagine, I almost choked! When I finally got my wits about me, and said "Hello", our precious Lord spoke to the man, "Son, behold your new wife!" God is a romantic; after all, it is He who invented romance! I urge you, let God pick your spouse and let Him introduce you at the proper time! He does do it so romantically! Just keep praying for your future spouse, and let God do the rest!

We spoke for a week on the phone every night knowing that this was who God in His great design planned to be our spouse! What did he look like? What did he do for a living? You can just imagine the questions we had about each other! Yet I was finding that I was falling for this "man"—this one that God had chosen just for me! Then on top of that, him for me! Marriage in the end is supposed to do one thing! Glorify GOD!!! When a husband and wife come together in this dark world, they should be—a snap-shot, if you will, of who God is! God in His great wisdom chose us out of everyone in the world to be husband and wife! Wow—this was going to be wonderful! I met my two future children (there are really no such things as steps in God's kingdom) and I met my future husband's parents! He met my children and most of us were really excited that we were going to be a "whole family." And life was a dream! In my mind, it was such a beautiful dream! We would march out together hand in hand fulfilling a call on our lives for the Lord to be glorified! If you have not realized it by now, I need to inform you that every dream usually ends with an alarm clock buzzing! Guess what, ours was about to buzz!

We had a whirlwind three-month courtship. When I went to my pastor to ask for a meeting with my future husband and myself, he was furious! He told me, "I will meet with you! My pastor, met with me first alone and gave me the drill! He was protecting my children and me because he knew what we had just walked through. My ex-husband had walked out on us three times in one year's time! He once told me that he was walking out on me not the children. But when you walk out of a marriage, you are destroying the very security your children have. You are walking out on more than just your spouse! You are walking out on God, the children and your spouse! You really need to realize that you will be held accountable to God for that. The vows you made before God and man He holds accountable!

My future husband and I prayed and asked, "Lord if this marriage is of you, then make my pastor OK with this." It was one of the fleeces I put out before the Lord to make sure this was of HIM! Once he asked me all the questions and I was able to answer them, even to my surprise, then he agreed to meet with my future husband and myself. I knew then that this was indeed God! I had to have the blessing of my pastor. God places us under people to protect us not to harm us and control us! My pastor was a great protector and a dear friend! Our wedding day was wonderful—people who were there said there was a spirit of joy and celebration that they had not experienced in any other marriage! Expectance was high because we knew this was of God. Everyone helped and brought food and celebrated what God had done! Our Father was taking two broken families and making one "whole" family out of it! We could not wait! What a joy it would be!

I do not know if you have ever seen something rebuilt, but most times, rebuilding resembles destruction! Have you ever noticed that God does not tell us all the details! HE always tells us the beautiful beginning and end of something but always leaves out all the in betweens! That is where the test of trusting Him comes in. Do we really trust Him with all the details and rest in His presence knowing He will work it all out for our good and His great glory?

My husband and I both had delusions of grandeur of how a marriage should be. The problem was that we never shared it with each other. When I look back, I believe my husband thought I would just walk in and fill the void of his ex-wife and I thought that he would be like my ex-husband was before everything went crazy! WRONG!!!! Once the marriage ceremony was over and the honeymoon began, the alarm clock rang—loudly!!!!

It only took one day to find out that this was not going to be easy. My flesh that I thought I had a handle on, rose up and let itself be made known to the whole world! My husband's flesh rose up too, and can I tell you, the two fleshes were not happy campers! A rude awakening was happening and I began thinking. *What on earth have I done!* But I knew this was God's will—even if we are in the center of God's will, we will have trouble. You see we have a couple of enemies! One great one from that day for a while was our flesh! Paul said it perfectly in Roman's 7:21-25:

> So I find this law at work; when I want to do good, evil is right there with me. For in my inner being I delight in God's law; but I see another law at work in the members of my body, waging war against the law of my mind and making me a prisoner of the law of sin at work within my members. What a wretched man I am! Who will rescue me from this body of death? Thanks be to God—through Jesus Christ our Lord! So then, I myself in my mind am a slave to God's law, but in the sinful nature a slave to the law of sin!

Who will deliver me from the body of death? Only as we die to our fleshly desires and give way to God's way for our lives will we walk in love, joy and His great peace! Remember what I said earlier: we do not grow in times of contentment; it is only through adversity and struggle of trials, tribulations, and contentions that we grow up in the Lord!

Never will I forget my pastor's question when we came back from the first week of our honeymoon. My husband and I went to Florida for a week alone, then we came back to pick up all four kids to go the mountains in Tennessee for another week! My dear pastor asked, "Well, dear, how is married life?"

My response was classic I believe! I told him, "You know pastor, I thought my flesh was under control, but that bugger rose up and is now alive and well on planet earth!" He laughed heartily! Then he told me something amazing! He said, "Dear, you would not have grown any further until you met your husband and this part of your flesh had been dealt with! You see, now God will do something great!"

Not long after we were married I was praying and the Lord spoke to me and said, "Child, I am using your family as training for what I have planned for you. Do not take the thing that you are going through lightly—they are training, purifying and preparing you for what is ahead!"

At the time I really did not want to know what was ahead, especially if this was training! One thing I have to say! We are now thirteen years later, it was hard, but all of it was worth it! There have been many great times and there have been many sorrowful times, but God has been there through every step we had taken. In the midst of heartache, God was the arms that held us through it all! He was the counselor, provider, healer of the broken, and when we walked through deep heartache of having to allow some of our children go, even if it meant letting them go to the pigs-pen, He was the one we could hold on to knowing He would keep them safe in the midst of it all! No matter what will happen to us, our children, our lives, we know His great Word that says He does make ALL things beautiful in its time! Through it all, we have learned something about ourselves, life, wisdom for this life, but most of all we learned something about our Lord and Savior! Every pig pen, every trial, tribulation, heartache, disappointment, and failure only caused me to draw closer and closer to the only one who KNEW what I was feeling inside! He never turned me away in frustration, disappointment or anger—on the contrary, He opened His loving arms and said, 'Child, I've been waiting for you to come in so I can comfort you and show you what you must do now!"

He will never leave us nor forsake us. We can run from Him and forsake Him, but He amazingly sits looking from the distance—for when we take that first step back toward Him, just like the prodigal son's father—He turns and runs toward us. Then He brings us His robe of righteousness, places a ring on our fingers, sandals on our feet and crowns on our heads, showing that we are His! There is nothing we can do that will turn Him away from us! He knows everything about us from the beginning to the end— every failure, every step, every success, and He is there in the middle of it all to rejoice with us when we succeed, cry with us when we hurt or fail, and comfort us, letting us know that He is a Father that so deeply loves us no matter what we may do or what we go through!

Rejoice, dear one, because your Father in Heaven loves you no matter what! HE is writing a beautiful story that is yours alone! If we let Him write it, it will truly be something beautiful that will shine for Him wherever we are!

The Blending

Chapter 3

Therefore since we are surrounded by such a great cloud of witnesses, let us throw off everything that hinders and the sin that so easily entangles and let us run with perseverance the race marked out for us. Let us fix our eyes on Jesus, the author and perfecter of our faith, who for the joy set before Him endured the cross, scorning its shame, and sat down at the right hand of the throne of God. Consider him who endured such opposition from sinful men, so that you will not grow weary and lose heart. (Hebrews 12:1-3)

I do not know who first coined the term "blended family," but whoever it was, they must have gotten a picture from the Lord about what it would be like! I love vinaigrette dressing. It is made in a blender. Each ingredient by itself is really not that good—but when you put all the ingredients together in the blender and mix it all together, it is incredible. That is what blending a family is like. Putting all the members in a blender and turning it on to make one unit! My husband and I both went through heartbreaking divorces that were not our choice. My ex-husband left because I became a Christian and changed, and my husband's ex-wife walked out on not only him, but Christianity too. Here we were two separate broken families that in God's design were going to become one! In blending you have to realize that brokenness has happened and all involved have been hurt. I believe if we could remember that, it would be a lot easier to blend. Unfortunately many times we are so involved with our own wounds that we cannot see that the other people are wounded too.

I had two children living with me, and we were neat, orderly, creative, independent, hyperactive, resourceful people. I raised my children to pick up after themselves and to always watch for what they could do to help others. The problem was if our "little part of the world" became disorderly or messy, we really had trouble handling it well. We were too orderly to sit back and have lots of fun. We did go on day trips to the beach—but thought better of spending too much money on vacations. I was a single parent with my own business trying to make it on one income.

My husband had two children and they lived for vacations. They were disorderly, messy, dependent, and a little lazy—they had all the time in the world for fun, fun, and more fun. Cleaning and making their world orderly and neat was a last priority—discipline was not part of their world either. The children had been through so much, and they were wounded when I met them. My husband is a good provider, but never worries about budgets, saving or if ends will be meet or not. Something will just happen and it will be all OK! Doesn't take effort on our part, it will just happen.

OK, we are on two different spectrums of the globe—, total polar opposites. I can just see our Lord in heaven saying to all the angels, "This is going to be dynamite!" Can I tell you it was! My husband is the grizzly Adams of our family. He enjoys tent camping, bathing in the creeks, no electricity; he can sit dirty for hours before ever thinking of taking a bath and thinks all of that is wonderful, coming back to nature. He would have loved to be born in the first century. I, on the other hand, am prim and proper; enjoy the comforts of things like showers, beds, baths, dry clothes, water and electricity. My idea of camping is at least a pop-up camper—but even that does not have a bathroom—therefore you have to make a hike every time you need the bathroom. Believe me at night that can get a little spooky! Do not get me wrong, I was raised in the country, on a farm until I was in the third grade. I remember picking cotton, picking pecans for Christmas money, shelling beans, harvesting corn, working in the field and riding on the tractor, feeding chickens and picking eggs. I came from hard-working stock—even fishing was for a purpose—food! Just to go off and take a walk for no reason and sleep in the woods for no reason except that you want to was beyond my understanding!

But here we are, God is the one who brought us all together and there was a purpose. Part of it was to chisel off the rough edges we both have and to learn to accept people right where they are! Was that easy—HEAVENS NO—actually it became war!!! As a matter of fact, we are still working on it, but it is so much better than it was before. As I stated earlier, blending is such a perfect word for the description of putting two people together that are total opposites, but just imagine, six people together that are opposites. There were many hard times, but when the times were good, it was awesome! I remember one of those precious times. We went camping at Cades Cove in Tennessee. There is no electricity or showers there. This is what they called roughing it, but this is what I called crazy—and this was my first time camping with my new family. Actually it was the second week after my husband and I got married. I really began to believe that God had just planted a cloud on top of our camp site. Everything was damp, our hair never dried, and bathing in the creek was horrible. That water was like ice! After the second day, my daughter and I decided we would stay dirty until we got home. The creek water was too cold. God does hear even those crazy cries in our hearts— because when we went to try to wash our hair in the bathroom sink (a big no no), a precious lady told us about showers in town for $2.00 each. We looked at each other and said, "Let's go, showers $2.00!"

I told my husband we were going take a hot shower in town, and believe me, that was the most precious shower I had ever taken in the world. I just stood under that hot water in utter bliss! Amazing what we get thankful for when we do not have it for a while.

By the middle of that week, my nerves were frazzled. All night we listened to a wolf howling, therefore there was no sleeping. To top it off, it rained each day and my rope broke. I went in the tent to have a talk with our Father God. After I finished my complaining the Lord gently spoke to me and said, "Child, stop complaining, get out there and begin to see the beauty that is all around you. You will be amazed what has been right in front of your face." That day as we began to walk around the park, I noticed the river there—because of all the rain, the river was rushing with such strength and velocity all I could do is sit in awe. I began to realize what that river was capable of doing with the power that was there because of all the rain. The flowers around were incredible—lavished by the rain that they were able to drink from. The rain never stopped the animals that were around—, the deer kept eating and now had drink because the rivers were filled, the squirrels were still stealing people's food and chips—life continued in spite of the storms and in spite of my attitude. When we focus on what we are missing, **we lose**—we lose the big picture of what God is trying to teach us through the storms. One of my favorite pictures is a picture I took on that day. Two trees were standing together like a frame, with the river rushing. Then a mist from the water was floating up. It was incredible to realize that the hand that made those trees, the river and water, was the same hand that made me. I think it was then I understood the scripture that says, for since the creation of the world God's invisible qualities—His eternal power and divine nature—have been clearly seen, being understood from what has been made, so that men are without excuse. (Ro 1:20) You see creation itself declares that there is a God! The amazing thing is that creation has no legs to take the good news, no mouth to speak the good news, no arms to reach out to hold a hurting soul, no eyes to shine the light of His love and no heart to understand, but we have all of that and so much more. If we let Him in to fully take over our lives and give Him total access to our heart then we have that ability to take Him everywhere we go. The hard part is that we must die so that He can live in us! When my husband and I got married, neither of us realized that it began the process of our dying not only as persons, but as independent entities. We were to become one flesh that would go and show a picture of who Jesus is to a world that is hurting and dying. It is a world that Jesus desires to touch.

Death hurts—and you know what, Jesus knows that better than any of us. All you have to do is look at what He went through from Gethsemane to the cross. He never said that we could not run to Him when we hurt, actually that is the very thing we need to do. Why do we run to everyone else but Him? We run to our friends to get their opinion but not to godly counsel. Could it be because we really do not want to hear what He has to say? We want our own way and our excuses to make it look like it is everyone else, not us. Maybe He will tell you to stop complaining and you change—instead of His changing the situation or other people. Blending is painful, but necessary. Dying is painful but also necessary. Remember, in John 12:24 scripture says, I tell you the truth, unless a kernel of wheat fall to the ground and dies, it remains only a single seed. But if it dies, it produces many seeds. If we allow our lives to die, and let our Gardener plant us, He will produce in us 50, 60 even 100 times the fruit that only one seed could produce. Just think if we know Him as Lord, we will spend eternity in Heaven with each other—we need to learn to love each other now and leave the work of changing others to the very capable hands of the Potter, Jesus Christ!

Please do not misunderstand, when we are parents and our children are living under our roof, it is part of our responsibility that we will be held accountable to help mold and shape them. We are a picture of Jesus to them while they are young. Are we perfect? Heavens no, but we are to always point them to what the Father says in His word. We cannot make them follow Christ, that is entirely their decision and choice when they get older, but we are to speak truth to them even though they do not want to hear it—just as our Heavenly Father does to us as His children now. Then there may come a time when we have to let them go, just as the Father allowed us to go and fall on our face and end up in a pig-pen. Then they will learn wisdom—the hard way—and come back. The key is when they come back, to embrace them just as the Father did. As Solomon said in Ecclesiastes 12:13 (NKJV)

Let us hear the conclusion of the whole matter. Fear God and keep His commandments, for this is man's all. For GOD will bring everywork into judgment, including every secret thing, whether good or evil.

Maybe you are doing some "blending" now in your life. Take it from one is has been and is still being blended, the bottom line is love! What is love? It is exactly what Jesus did on the cross! HE loved us so much He was willing to die for us. Are we willing to love others by dying to ourselves and our desires and allowing others to be who God created them to be? In other words, are we willing to forget what "we NEED" and give our spouses or children what THEY desperately need? Remember it is not our job to mold or change others, although God does put iron that sharpens iron together. We must allow God to change them. Realize that you are iron that is sharpening each other and thank God for that part of your family member or spouse that sharpens you, and always remember to listen to each other. God may just speak to you through one of them. Love others as you would like them to love you. Scripture tells us that we reap what we sow, if we sow love, that is exactly what we will get back. Blending hurts because it involves dying, but when it is done, the taste, smell and refreshment of the ingredients blended together are outstanding. Do not give up in well doing, for in due season you **will** reap a harvest if you faint not!

Abrams Falls

Chapter 4

Hazards: slippery rocks when wet
Highlights: Creek and falls

> *I pray for those who will believe in me*
> *through their message, that all of them may*
> *be one. Father, just as you are in me and I*
> *am in you. May they also be in us so that the*
> *world may believe that you have sent me.*
> *(John 17:20b-21)*

Abram's Falls is a 5 mile hike from inside Cades Cove. The trailhead starts with a rustic log bridge built over a beautiful stream. You cannot help but notice the incredible clear running water of Abram's Creek. In the summer the waters invite hikers to come put their tired hot feet in so they can cool off. The river calls out, "Refreshing is here, come on in!" In the summer months it can be dry and thirsty, but at the same time a summer storm can come up within minutes and soak you before you know what is happening. I do not think I will ever forget my first time hiking Abram's Falls. It was a wonderful day—the sun was shining and I could not wait to check out the river that ran on the side of the trail and the falls at the end of the hike. We had heard that because of the storm the night before, the falls were unbelievable! Our children ranged from age seven to seventeen and I wondered if the younger ones would be able to make the 5 mile hike. We knew it had a slight incline, but those can be the most tiresome. I had packed plenty water and beef jerky and snacks for the trip up so I felt we would be OK—but 5 miles, that kept going through my mind. Sometimes, we need to just forget how long the journey may be and just enjoy, otherwise we miss the scenery along the way.

The first thing we encountered once we crossed the little bridge was a beautiful forest and trail that was canopied over with lush green trees. It was like walking in a dream we had just entered a whole different world. Here we were protected. The sun was not beating down on us, and we were covered by the shade of the trees. At the same time we were cooled by the running creek and the breeze that came from it. In our journey with the Lord, He does the same thing. He covers us continuously with His loving kindness, mercy and grace, and then cools us by the washing of the water of His wonderful Word.

As we were walking and singing, suddenly out of the thick forest a deer ran out and stopped right in front of me. Both of us were in total shock—for a moment neither of us moved—then the deer looked over at the creek. He turned from me and ran down into the creek and put his whole head down in the water to drink and cool off. There is a scripture that says, "As the deer pants for the steams of water so my soul pants for you, O God. My soul thirsts for God for the living God." Psalm 42:12. That deer forgot about all fear of man. He did not care that someone happened to trespass into his world, because his desperate need of that living water was so strong. But not only did he just drink—he dunked his whole head into the water. When we begin this journey with the Lord, we cannot come into it half way or hap-hazard—each of us have got to jump in with both feet and dunk our head and heart into all that is of God! We cannot allow fear to stop us or turn us from our desired goal. We must desire more of Him no matter the cost, more than anything else in our world.

I could not get that sight out of my head—and yet I could not wait to see what else God had for us to learn on the hike up. Remember, my husband and I were in good shape, my 14- and 17- year olds were also able, but we had younger ones with us and we would have to help them along the way. There were places on the trail that were very slippery because of the rains the night before therefore we had to watch that the two younger ones were able to pass in safety. Many times we had to stop and rest to allow them to regain strength and get some water and nourishment. They began to get tired and the incline was a bit steeper than we realized. One thing we found in some hiking books. The people who write these books are experienced hikers, therefore, when they say it is an easy or moderate or strenuous hike, it is by their standards, not ours! Abram's Falls was considered a moderate hike, therefore we thought, *Well that won't be too bad.* We were wrong! As young ones often do, they began to get tired and complain. God reminded me of some songs I used to sing with my children. "I can do anything, can do, anything through Him, can do, anything through Him who gives me strength, I can do anything." As we began to sing and encourage each other, — it was amazing how we worked together and actually began having a great time. We were not fighting against each other or wondering what we had done to deserve all of this, but we began to realize that we needed each other and that we could indeed encourage one other. Then as boys/men often do, they needed to compete. The girls against the boys—this stopped them from thinking about how hard it was and began causing them to concentrate on the goal—getting to the falls first safely. What a great time of enjoyment when we got there. The amazing thing about the falls is that you can hear them long before you can see them. Especially because of the storm the night before, the water was gushing with such mighty power it was breathtaking. We picked a spot and made a picnic with our snacks, drinks and thanked God for getting us there safely. We have a goal as Christians also, that goal is the prize of the high calling in Christ Jesus! If we keep our eyes fixed on that goal and desire everyone to get there, I believe there would be a lot less competition in the body of Christ and a whole lot more love. We are in this together. Let's keep our eyes fixed on Jesus. Also fix them on our brothers and sisters and how we can help them make the journey safely.

The children loved exploring the whole area and climbing on everything they could. There was no fear in these kids about heights, sharp cliffs, or the rushing water. They were determined to experience everything they could and their competition became cruel. They suddenly stopped working with each other and began to work against each other. When we play games and get on the defense, then expect an offense to rise up. They had gotten to their goal, therefore all else was forgotten.

Suddenly I looked up at those powerful falls and realize that all that water was traveling in the same direction. Because it was all headed for the same goal, it was powerful, but if you put different avenues for it to travel, it would no longer be so powerful. So many times God places people together so that they can be powerful working together, but then they all begin to have their own agendas. The sad thing is that things get accomplished, but not as profoundly as they could have if all would have worked together in unity.

How good and pleasant it is when brothers (and sisters) dwell together in unity! It is like precious oil poured on the head, running down on the beard, running down on Aaron's beard, down upon the collar of His robes. It is as if the dew of Hermon were falling on Mount Zion. For there the Lord bestows his blessing, even life forevermore. (Psalm 133NIV)

Let us strive to get along and work together instead of fighting against each other. How can we love if we are fighting! Abram's Falls always reminds me of those wonderful lessons: Always be thirsty for more and more of the Lord and the life He has given us, just like the deer thirst for the streams of water; then always have compassion for the weaker vessels and work together in love and unity. After all, it is there where the blessing of the Lord will flow!

Once we sat and rested next to the river, we could not help but be refreshed! We would take off our hiking boots and wade in the cooling river, letting it wash away all the tiredness of the trip up the mountain down to the falls.

We were then ready to make the trip back! The nourishment, rest and enjoyment of the river gave us a fresh new start. We were ready to take on what was next, the trip back! The Word of God is like that river! As we sit and wade in its refreshing waters daily, we are ready for the journey we have to take that day. We could stand the cold of the river water, by sitting in the sun. Then we could allow the river to wash the sweat, dust, and stench off of us from the hike up. Then when we got out of the river, we would feel clean. The Word of God is like that too. In Ephesians 5:25-26 it says, Husbands, love your wives, just as Christ loved the church and gave himself up for her to make her holy, cleansing her by the washing with water through the word, and to present her to himself as a radiant church, without stain or wrinkle or any other blemish, but holy and blameless. The Word removes all the dust and sweat and junk we pick up each day and allows us to start fresh and clean. His mercies are new every morning!

It always amazes me how much shorter the trip back seems than the trip there. Maybe it is because once you have made the trip there, you know what to expect on the way back. Because of where we have been, we are able to help those who are just starting this wonderful walk and adventure of the Christian walk. It is not a sprint, it is a marathon! It is not for the faint at heart—it is for those who will walk with faith! I got a kick out of our children. When we would pass up hikers that were headed to the falls, they would always ask, "How much further to the falls?" My kids were so quick to encourage them, "You are almost there, just over that hill." Or further down the trail they would tell the passing hikers, "The falls are worth the trip; they are beautiful! Keep going, do not give up." That is exactly what we are to do with each other. Once we have made the trip, we know how incredible the lesson we learned was and how worthy the goal is. It was worth every tiring, hard and dangerous step. Once we made it to the end we were able to stop and rest our feet once again in the river that ran under the rustic log bridge. Then we would laugh and reminisce over every beautiful thing we saw. It was quite amazing just how quickly we forgot the rough times—but we could never forget the beautiful falls that were our goal.

Once we get to heaven and see how incredible our Jesus is, we will realize how much it was worth every danger, every trial, every storm and every mountain! Keep your heart focused on the Lord, your life's goal.

As a prisoner for the Lord, then, I urge you to live a life worthy of the calling you have received. Be completely humble and gentle; be patient, bearing with one another in love. Make every effort to keep the unity of the Spirit through the bond of peace. (Ephesians 4:1-3NIV)

Rainbow Falls

Chapter 5

Hazards: Rock slippery especially around falls, fog
              in bad weather
Highlights: Rainbow Falls, wildflowers

*Now we see but a poor reflection as in a
mirror; then we shall see face to face. Now I
know in part; then I shall know fully, even as
I am fully known. (1Corinthians 13:12)*

The human mind is so amazing! It never ceases to
amaze me how we as humans tend to forget the
hard things and only remember the good. Like child-
birth—we do not remember the labor pains once we
see that beautiful bundle God has blessed us with.
All the pain, sorrow and agony are forgotten. At once
we realize that it was all worth it to have the incredible package we hold in our arms.

Rainbow Falls is a 5.6 mile hike to the falls that has a stiff incline, but once you reach the falls, it is unbelievable. At certain times of the day, when the sun shines on the falls a rainbow appears. The sight is spectacular! Rainbow Falls is actually the half way point up Mount LeCount. There is a hotel on top of this mountain that you hike to and sleep over night. The hike all the way to the hotel is very steep. Supplies are brought to the hotel by either lama or a helicopter. Just imagine the hike there. Rainbow Falls is located right in the middle of Gatlinburg, Tennessee. You veer off on Roaring Fork Road located by a park in the middle of the city and enter into a whole new world! It is like being transformed into a different time zone. A time when life was slower, simple and hard, yet people knew what was important. God, family and community— they all needed each other and were there for each other. Unlike today, where people are independent, doing their own thing with no thought about their neighbors. Today people tend to be more self-focused than God and neighbor focused. The trip there always reminded me this is what we need— to come back to basics of life, to what is really important. When it's all said and done, the thing that will matter is our relationship with God, family and others. That is the only thing that will remain and what we will be judged for.

Because of the moisture from rain and the thickness of the woods, the trail can be quite foggy. The second time we hiked this trail was one of those days. I forgot about the continued incline of the hike, the length of over two miles up to the falls, and the fog that can occur! With each hike there are dangers, just like with each journey in life, there can be dangers if you are not prepared for them.

As we began this hike, the forest was incredible. Already there was a promise of the possible sighting of bears, deer and beautiful wildflowers. The sun was totally blocked from view because of the dense forest, and at the beginning of the hike, a beautiful little creek ran through. The sound from that running water is so peaceful. It just calls to you, "Come sit a while and think about all the blessings you have." How many of us are too busy to stop and take a walk through the woods? Wow—coming back to that resting time realizing there is a God who created all of this! The hike was uneventful for quite some time. Then the incline and altitude began to take a toll on everyone. We had to stop and rest several times and because the altitude was higher than what we were used to in Louisiana, but of course, any altitude is higher than what we are used to! So many times in our journey of life, when we get tired, we do need to just take a rest—sit a spell enjoy the scenery and realize once again what is really important! Not all the hustle and bustle of life, the go, go, go mentality, but a mentality that says let us sit a spell and rest. If we never stop, the anger, frustration, the disappointments and stress of daily life will finally take over. God designated a Sabbath day rest for the children of Israel. The Sabbath day rest was made for man to reflect and remember God, family, community, and the things that are important to God and should be priority for us! It was also designed to take into account just how blessed we are and that there is a God in heaven looking out for us. He knew that we needed rest; we needed time to set apart and remember who He is and what He has done for us. After all, He sent His only Son, Jesus to die for us. A dear friend told me years ago a very special gold nugget that I have always kept dear. God gently leads, Satan shoves and pushes. That is how you know you are being led by God or pressured by Satan's schemes. When I sit back and consider the birds of the air, the flowers of the fields and see that our Heavenly Father takes care of them and that not a bird falls from the sky that He does not know about it, it reminds me, I have nothing to worry about! He is here, watching, protecting, loving and teaching me. He created everything I am looking at and experiencing and He created it for my enjoyment and provision! WOW! We need to have a day just to realize that, and then we will know we are deeply loved by our Creator!

As we continued up to the falls, the fog began to come in. Some of the trail is very narrow, and there are spots of serious drop off. There were points in the trail that the trees would overhang and create an arch—it was so incredible. In the middle of the fog, everything became more alive and rich. We were hiking during the fall of the year and the leaves were orange, yellow and some were still green, but the colors mixed were like a painting portrayed by a master. The sights were incredible, but the air, was thick with the dampness from the fog.

Fog is one thing that we are used to here in Louisiana. It is not uncommon for it to be so foggy that we cannot see the house across the street. In 1 Corinthians 13:12 (NIV) says, Now we see but a poor reflection as in a mirror; then we shall see face to face. I have always taken fog to be just like we see things today. We never see clearly what is really going on until we can look back and realize God had a message in that situation.

God allows "foggy" times in our lives for us to learn some very important things. When I was driving to work one day, the fog was so thick, yet I could see the sun shining through. It was not bright, but I knew it was the sun. Suddenly I realized that many times God allows us to walk through some foggy times to be able to shine the light of His love to a lost and dying world around us. We are lights shining in darkness saying, "This is the way, walk here in it with us." (See Isaiah 30:21) It is the same way in our journey of life.

We are to shine our light before men that they would see our good works and glorify our God! (Matthew 5:16) When we get caught up in this world activities going here and there, we lose the very thing that makes life wonderful—time together that we spend sharing, talking, laughing enjoying each other and remembering the good things instead of concentrating on all the "stuff" going on in life. We lose our joy, peace and love that would be the very things that draw people to us. We do have rocky times and storms we must go through, but that's it. We go through them, we do not stay in them unless we so choose! But in the middle of them, God in His goodness fills us with His grace that enables us to go through them. So many of us walk in the fog believing we see clearly, but in essence we are seeing things through veiled eyes and a veiled heart. Our fog can be a fog of fear, a fog of rejection, a fog of condemnation, fog of the past or we can look clearly and see our God!

We finally made a clearing, and behold, before our faces was a view that was unbelievable. We could see for miles and the amazing thing that was right behind us was the fog! But here, where we were standing, a breeze had blown the fog away! It reminded me of the old song:

> I can see clearly now the rain is gone—
> I can see ALL obstacles in my way.
> Gone are the dark days that had me bound—
> It is gonna be a bright, bright sun shiny day!
>
> I think I can make it now, the pain is gone
> All of the bad feelings have disappeared,
> Here is the rainbow I've been praying for
> It's gonna be a bright, bright sun-shinny day
>
> Look all around there's nothing but blue skies,
> Look straight ahead there's nothing but blue
>   skies!
> *(Johnny Nash, 1972 hit song)*

Amazingly those days do come to pass and not to stay! When it all passes, the views of our lives are outstanding! Then we begin to see clearly and understand! He is God and I am not!

As we continued up the rest of the climb, we did see deer and a mama bear and her cubs. There was no fear, they were so beautiful and they just went on by like we weren't there. Then there it was the sounds of the falls! We could hear them, but could not see them yet! That is faith, knowing it is right there ahead! When we turned the last bend to the falls, there they were right past the bridge! Now the bridge consisted of a log and below that bridge was a long drop off with the river running down! Imagine just how narrow that bridge was! It was the size of a large log; we had to trust that it would hold us! But right across that bridge was our conquest, our goal, the beauty of it all was right in front of our faces. If we gave into fear of crossing that bridge, we could only gaze at the falls from a far, but we could not go and experience them first hand. We still had to climb some very slippery logs and rocks to get to them, but that was a piece of cake—we had the right equipment in our hiking boots! In our spiritual walk with God I have seen many stop right there! You see, fear only comes to pull you back and push you back. Fear only stops you from taking a chance and conquering the very fear you face. You know, fear of falling, fear of failure it just stops you right there dead in your tracks—you never go forward! That bridge is the bridge to new beginnings! You see, He is a God of new beginnings—He makes a way where there seems to be no way. He delights when His children trust Him to see them through the journeys. He will never disappoint us, but He will take great joy watching us get overwhelmed over the things He has for us! We are to never fret; He has our best in mind. If we never step onto the bridge and cross it, we will miss out on what God has for us! Dear one, step over and see what He has waiting for you on the other side! There is a scripture that I love in Song of Solomon 2:11-12

See. The winter is past; the rains are over and gone. Flowers appear on the earth; the season of singing has come. The cooing of doves is heard in our land.

He is a God of new beginnings—step over and watch Him move! It just takes a step of faith to believe Him instead of the lie you have entertained in your mind! Believe!

Once the Lord spoke to me through a trial and asked me, "Child, what did you go to see on top of this last mountain? Was it the view or was it who I was? When I am lifted up in a situation, everything else pales in comparison. When you fail is when you lift the circumstances and failures up instead of real-izing that in spite of the circumstances and failures of the past, present and future I AM! If you begin to seek me and lift me up, you will find ME. Then I can use the past, present, and future for your good and My glory!" In God's kingdom, it is never too late—each day is a new beginning, if we would only train our minds to lift Him up instead of the circumstances or failures of the past and present! But I when I am lifted up from the earth, will draw all men unto myself. The bottom line is whose report will you believe? Israel stayed in the desert 40 years because they believed the lies and refused the truth. Because of their unbelief and their wishy washy attitude He could do nothing through them. The only thing He could do was to sustain them in the center of their desert and wilderness "they chose" to stay in. It is not about who we are or what we do, how old we are or how young we are, it is all about who HE is and who we allow Him to be in our lives. We must focus on Him, forgetting what is behind and straining toward what is ahead, I press on toward the goal to win the prize for which God has called me heavenward in Christ Jesus. (See Philippians 3:14) That day for us it was the falls—we crossed that bridge and was it ever worth it! We were able to sit and enjoy the cool breezes from the falls, watch the sun come across that water and create an incredible rainbow. We ate, drank and were refreshed so we were well able to make the journey down the mountain! What we experienced there we took with us in our hearts and shared it with those we came in contact with! To this day, I still recommend the hike at Rainbow Falls because of what we experienced there! When we come down from each one of our spiritual "mountain" trips we are to take with us what we learned to a hurting world and share that there is indeed One who is high and lifted up! He is our God who watches over us to protect and nurture us. Trust in Him dear friend! Remember His beautiful words in Proverbs 3:5-6 (NKJV)

Trust in the Lord with all your heart, and lean not unto your own understanding. In all your ways acknowledge Him and He shall direct your paths!

Tremont Logging Trail

Chapter 6

Hazards: Slippery road when wet
Highlights, creek, wildflowers and views

> *Trust in the Lord with all your heart and lean*
> *not on your own understanding; in all your*
> *ways acknowledge him, and he will make*
> *your paths straight. (Proverbs 3:5-6)*

Tremont Logging Trail is a road that leads up
to the Tremont Trail where there are cascades
of waterfalls and forests that are amazing. In 1994
there was a series of torrential storms and down-
pours that eventually caused the destruction of the
road leading up to the trailhead. Cars were unable
to drive up because of the complete destruction to
the road. I have never seen the devastation of an
earthquake first hand, but I believe that this is what

it would look like! Who would ever know that water had that kind of power coming down a mountain! There we were—we heard about the cascades and the trail how beautiful they were. There was none to compare to them. My husband's desire was to see the cascades coming down the mountain—therefore, thus began our hike! My husband is not one to listen to warning, and when he decides to do something there is nothing that will stop him. As many of us do, he learns the hard way!

Have you ever begun a project and in the middle of it wondered if you were completely insane to have been talked into it? Well, this is what it felt like on our first experience of Tremont Logging Trail! We started walking up the "road" that was created for cars and trucks, hoping that the hike would not be too long! This was our first mistake. We did not realize that the "road" was approximately two miles long up hill and that was on a good day, when the road was intact. Here at the beginning, the road looked passable and we thought we could do it! Please hear me, when people put a road block closing something off, it is for a very good reason! They know something you do not and they are only trying to protect you from what is ahead! When I think about our walk with God, how many times has God placed a "road block" in the way of something that I thought seemed OK later to find out that it was NOT OK! As a matter of fact, the road-block was there for my protection. Amazingly, God lets us learn from our mistakes, and only says, "OK are you ready to do it MY way?" What an incredible God of mercy and grace! The problem was that I was about to learn that I needed to have more mercy and grace with others too.

Here we went, starting up the logging road singing and checking out everything around us! As we went forward, I began to notice cracks developing in the road. I asked my husband, "What do you think these are from?" He then told me about the storms that had passed through. The park ranger already told him that the storms had damaged the road so a car was not able to go through. OK, so what, a car could not go through, but surely people could! Every step we took became more and more dangerous, and the cracks became bigger and bigger until they became major craters! Let me tell you, the moon had nothing on this "road." I began to be concerned with the two little ones. We had to pick them up over some of the huge cracks and damage in the road. As we kept going up, I was astounded at the fact that the creek alongside the "road" did not even seem to be affected. The water kept going down in such an amazing beauty — and the sound of the water was intoxicating. Several times we sat down on the side of what used to be a road and just listened to the sound and beauty of that creek water flowing down the mountain. That water had one destination, going down to water the valley in which people lived! What an incredible journey it took! As I began to look around, I saw how many trees were downed because of the rushing water from the storm. They added to the damage of the road. Also, much of the dirt that created the creek side was washed away into the creek. All the creek did was carry all the trash that had been dumped into it by the storm down to the valley. It never held onto it. It just let it flow down. I sat and thought about that for a while listening to the beautiful sound of the water flowing down, and I suddenly realized. God desires that we become just like that creek. Through the storms in our lives, He desires us to just allow all the junk that tries to get dumped into our lives to flow downhill. We have a job to do! We are to be lights and salt to a world that is dying and in terrible shape. If we keep trying to handle all the debris that comes into our lives, we will never be able to do what God has called us to do. If we hold onto it, we will become a polluted stream—one that people cannot drink from.

I realized also that the road was created by man. When the storm came, the road was unable to withstand the power and force of the storm so it crumbled. It reminded me of the story in the Bible about the house built on sand and the house built on the rock! OK, this is a creek, but it has the same implications. Whatever "we" build, will be destroyed in the storms of our lives, but what God builds will last forever! Ecclesiastes 3:14 (NKJV) says:

> "I know that whatever God does, it shall be forever. Nothing can be added to it and nothing taken from it. God does it that men should fear before Him."

Why are we so surprised when storms come? In this world we will have trouble, Jesus said in John 16:33 (NKJV), But be of GOOD cheer, for I have overcome the world! (Emphasis added.) Looking at that creek, I noticed that it did not look worried, troubled, confused and weary; it just kept doing what God had designed it to; flowing down! It never stopped to ask what should I do, and it did not call all the friends it knew to see what it needed to do—it just kept flowing! *Wow*, I thought, *how profound.* When storms come into our lives, do we stop and try to figure out what is going on, or do we just keep flowing in God's river of love for us! You see, there is a river that runs from the throne of God that is the river of love for us—it is crimson because this river is the blood of Jesus! What a cost He paid for us—He gave it all because of His great and abounding love for us! When things happen, do we think that He has lost control for a moment or maybe He has taken a vacation—or gone to get a drink! NO, He is completely in control and He knows what He is doing—He is working all things for our good, and do not forget, for His glory and also to conform us to the image of Jesus! These storms are just there to conform us—not destroy us! There is a scripture that I love in Job 23:10 (NIV) it says:

> But He knows the way that I take; and when
> He has tested me, I will come forth as gold.

One translation's commentary says that He was not punishing Job, on the contrary, He was just putting him on display for others to see the gold that had been refined in his life—and to show glory to his God! Sometimes when "storms" come in our lives,

God desires us to just show Him glory by trusting Him and letting it all flow down! I do not know about you, but I desire to be like that creek! The sounds from that creek were so peaceful and incredible. When storms come into our lives, do people hear peace and a trusting attitude from our mouths or do they hear fear, anger, unforgiveness and bitterness! Remember out of our belly flows rivers of life or death. The Jewish belief is that the belly and heart were one in the same. To know what was in your heart/belly, all you had to do was listen to yourself. There is an old phrase that says garbage in garbage out— good in and good out.

You see, out of the abundance of the heart— the mouth speaks! Matthew 12:35 (NKJV) I have learned to listen to myself and what I am saying. When I am dealing with a situation, what comes out of my mouth? Whatever I hear is what is in my heart! Am I trusting and flowing in the love of my God, or am I fretting in a river polluted with garbage from a storm? John 16:33(NIV) says, I have told you these things so that in me you may have peace, in this world we will have trouble, but be of good cheer, because Jesus has overcome the world! We have no reason to fret—after all, if God is for us, who can be against us? When this happens in our lives, we need to jump into that crimson river and allow Him to wash away all the guilt, condemnation, hurt, fear and sin from our lives and remember that when He was nailed to that cross; our rap sheet was completely wiped clean by His blood! You have a new beginning—a new way of living—choose not to go back to the old way of life!

As we continued a big further, we noticed that trees and the road were not the only tragedies; many animals were killed also! On the "road" I noticed a bird—I could not understand, he had the ability to fly, why then did he fall and die! As I was considering this pitiful creature, I realized that not one bird falls that our Heavenly Father does not know of it! Sometimes, it is just their time to go. My grandfather died when I was in the third grade and it devastated me! He was such an incredible man—but that is another book! Sometimes we cause early deaths because of the way we take care of our bodies, but sometimes it is just our time to go! Psalm 139 is one of my favorite Psalms! Verse 16 says:

"Your eyes saw my substance, being yet unformed. And in Your book they all were written, the days fashioned for me, when as yet there were none of them."

You see, God knew the last day of that precious beautiful little bird, and I bet all the things that bird was meant to accomplish here on earth were done! When its days were up, then the Lord allowed life to be taken from it here on earth! I do believe that birds and other animals will go to heaven too! Just my personal opinion! When the last day of my grandpa came, God took him home! After all, when it is time for one of your children to come home, aren't you ready for them too? We have a Father that loves us so much—and His heart yearns for us! And if we as humans long for our children, how much more does a perfect Father God! The problem is we are not ready to let them go! I remembered His beautiful Word as I looked at that little bird and realized that God was completely in control!

He even saw where we were there—very far away from the main road and our vehicle! Because the "road" was becoming more and more dangerous, my husband made the decision that we should start back! I tell you, I do not know if it was the incredible beauty of the creek, all the lessons I was learning, or being concerned with the younger ones, but I had no idea how far we had traveled! The trail back seemed to get longer and longer! The kids began to complain and I tell you I was not far behind them! In my mind I was thinking—*This man is crazy? To take four kids and his wife that was defiantly not prepared for this; so far!*

Have you ever heard of those warnings on TV? *For the next 60 seconds we will be conducting a test. It is only a test of the broadcasting system.* Well, this was a test—for the next however long, I was undergoing a test, and I can tell you, I was not passing it! I wasn't saying anything **yet**, but boy, can I tell you it was at the tip of my tongue! Because of the danger of the road, everything took so much longer, and I was wondering why we had gone so far in this dangerous situation! OK—I snapped and said it! "You must be crazy—why would you take us on such an "adventure?" How long will this be?" All of us were tired, hot, beginning to be very thirsty, because we ran out of water, big mistake, the kids were complaining—you get the picture!

When I was about to speak again, the Lord told me to be quiet and pray. Boy, can I tell you my lips got a life unto themselves and I blew it! Heat, thirst and weariness will do things to you—it makes this critter come out in you. I believe the Bible calls it the "carnal man." That booger rises up when you least expect it and wham, he takes over totally! Out of my mouth came this complaining and I- told- you so attitude! "Did you not see the road block? We were not even supposed to go this way! How much longer is it anyway?" I told my husband and gave him a piece of my mind. Well, I won't tell you what piece. That critter came out of me and jumped on him, and then it jumped into the kids too! We were having one fit of flesh all over the place!

The Lord broke into all the loud junk and said, "Child of mine, I told you to pray—ask me for a way to make it down."

Once I took about twenty deep breaths in order to pray—you know one of those prayers you think God is not hearing! I prayed, Lord *Help us down this mountain—we are so tired and I really don't know if we can make it down. HELP!!!* Well, about five minutes later we began to hit the area of the road that was at least passable, and here came a truck out of the woods! He was a park ranger and asked us first what we were doing there and explained that that was exactly what the road blocks were for! Then he asked if we would like a ride down.

That day I found out that God can deal with "issues" a lot better than I can—and in a much gentler way. He will deal with it in a loving and gentle manner—in a way that we will never forget those life's lessons. Then in the midst of it, He will not allow us to be tempted beyond what we can handle! I should have given my husband more grace and trusted God a whole lot more. That day I learned that the WILL of GOD will never lead you where the GRACE of God cannot keep you. He knows what He is doing in our lives, and I tell you, I am still learning! But I do know this, we reap what we sow I need so much grace; and I know others need that grace too. I have in no way "arrived." I am still learning, and I praise God that He has grace with me and even at times, I am sure, chuckles at some of my goof ups. We cannot love people truly until we come to a place of even laughing at ourselves and our fellow man! I don't see anyone floating around in white robes with wings here on earth—our robes and crowns will not be given to us until we get to Heaven! The one thing I do desire is that daily I would die more and more so that He can live more and more in and through me! There are times when God will allow us to journey with others for them to learn some powerful lessons—then there will be times when others will journey with us to learn our lessons! Let us all deal kindly with each other and learn just like that creek to let it all flow downhill! I desire a stream to flow out of my belly that others desire to drink from. In order to have that type of stream, I must allow the junk just to flow down and away. Then others will desire to have what God has placed within me!

I want to jump into the river and flow!

Tremont Cascades Trail

Chapter 7

Highlights: Cascades of water and lush forest
Hazards: Muddy trail after rain

*There is a time for everything, and a season
for every activity under heaven: (Ecclesiastes
3:1)*

On the way to Cades Cove four miles up a
road right outside of the town of Townsend,
Tennessee is the trailhead of Tremont Cascades. It
is the same road that had been destroyed by a flood
that was mentioned in the previous chapter. Praise
the Lord; it was repaired by the time we went back
the next year! Once we got to the beginning of the
trailhead we parked in a beautiful forest area. When
we got there, we saw many horse trailers because the
trail is known as an exciting horse trail. There is a

sense of excitement already in the air. All the way up the road to the trailhead runs the creek! On the trip up the mountain it is not unlikely to see, deer, geese, amazing wild flowers and hear the sound of the water all the way up! Rolling down our windows in our car, the sound was amazing! It is such a sound of peacefulness even though at times it may become very loud! If one gets in a reclining position by the creek, it is just a matter of time before he drifts off to sleep! This is what it is like when we come and sit by the river of God's love. There was such a sense of peace that all our cares just fell away and we began to realize that there was nothing to worry about! By the time we got to the trailhead, we could not wait! We were pumped with excitement waiting to see what else could possibly be there. All the way up, we stopped several times to take pictures! With all of us in the vehicle, each one shouting, "Look at this—oooh look at that—wow, did you see that?" As you can imagine, as soon as the car stopped—all six of us jumped out ready for what was ahead! In order to get on any trail, we had to make sure we had all the gear we needed—hiking boots, water, snacks, picnic supplies, hats, mosquito spray, whatever we thought we might need we carried! Now we were ready! Let's go!

The first thing you see as you head for the trailhead is this beautiful little bridge. In order to get to the trailhead you have to cross the bridge over the river. The river is traveling very fast at this point because you are far up the mountain. Already the cascades are amazing—and that is just at the bridge. Once you cross the bridge and the amazing river, you see the most beautiful sight you can imagine! Just imagine seeing a forest with amazing wildflowers everywhere growing on the sides of the mountains next to the river. At this point we were not walking next to the river—it begins to get farther from the trail because of the forest. The Cascades are amazing, and just when you think, you could not possibly see any more beautiful and powerful waterfalls, WHAM, another one comes into view! On this particular trail the sights, sounds and feeling is like none other I have experienced! *I believe that God said in his heart, I am going to amaze my children with my creativity! I'll create this river in the middle of nowhere and put cascades of water all the way down to give drink to them and to refresh them in the midst of this thick forest!* And as you know, there it was! HE spoke and it came into being! Wow!!! Everything is so beautiful! The dense forest and lush green trees and bushes tend to invite you in— *Come explore, come see what God has done!* All the way up, there are amazing wildflowers just dancing in the breeze created by the river. As you walk, the sun shines through the trees creating an atmosphere of glory! As you continue on the journey, you just KNOW He is right there with you enjoying your amazement of all He has done! The presence of the Lord is incredible, and I understand once again why there is a Sabbath day rest! There is no way that you can walk on this trail and not KNOW in your heart that there is a God is heaven that created all of this! Once when I was taking a picture of the cascades, a man came to stand next to me with his camera and tripod. I could not help myself—I began to speak of how awesome and amazing the sights and sounds there were! I asked no one in particular how anyone could not believe in God when they got a look at this creation. After all, if there is a creation, there has to be a Creator! I did not realize that this man was an atheist. He just sat and listened to me for a bit then said, "I have never thought of it in that aspect before. That is really something to consider!" How can some of the most simple things be right in front of our face, yet we never see them? Are we humans so blind?

When the children began to get hungry we found a place right by the cascades and made a picnic. Before we ate, we gave thanks to God for the privilege of coming to that place and allowing us to be nourished not only with food, but with the sounds and sights He had created for us to enjoy! Resting in His presence, eating and drinking, we were barely able to speak for the sounds of the waterfall and the beauty that surrounded us!

We have been there in spring, winter, fall, and summer and each season has its own amazing characteristics about it! Even in winter, the cascades are amazing. The life of that river in the midst of the dead is awe inspiring! The river never stops—throughout all the seasons it continues flowing—it is one thing we can always count on! Just like the river of God, it always is flowing there for us to come and drink from. His river I can bring with me everywhere I go. It is His wonderful love letters to me written in the Bible!

It was right here that the Lord began to speak to me about the seasons. We have seasons in our own lives. Each of us goes through the times of spring, summer, and fall then winter! Through these hikes and flower arranging, God has taught me a lot about the seasons of our lives. Each one is very important and we cannot skip any, we must go through them and embrace them as ordained by our Heavenly Father. You see, each season has its purpose in life. Just as Ecclesiastes 3:1 says:

There is a time for everything, and a season for every activity under heaven."

In Tremont spring is the time of many wildflowers. Every time you turn a corner there is a different type of flower—many of which I had never seen before. Each one is unique in its design and fragrance—each one is important and brings us great joy and hope! They turn the trail into a walk through a beautiful garden of rushing water and wildflowers!

The spring in our lives is a time of new birth—new beginnings! Everywhere we look there is new life, new sprouts; everything seems fresh and alive! The air is comfortable, not to cold and not too warm—it all seems just wonderful! Spring is when love seems to blossom the most—new spring love for the June weddings! It is where the seeds that have been planted suddenly begin to break forth in the ground and we see flowers then the promise of fruit to come! Everything that was dead seems to blossom overnight! There is hope in the air, hope of great things to come! God faithfully sends spring showers that we know will produce May flowers. We move from the inside to the outdoors—although much work needs to begin, it is quite pleasant, because you have the hope of what is to come! We are beginning to plant our flowerbeds, gardens, fertilizing our fruit trees, preparing for all the fresh fruits and vegetables to come in the summer. You cannot wait! There is such anticipation in the air—and we are just happy to be alive! School is about to finish and the hope of a full summer is at hand! Kids are excited, Easter comes and we remember what was done for us on the cross by Jesus! He was bruised for our iniquities, He was crushed for our sins, the punishment that gave us peace was upon Him, and by His stripes we are healed! (See Isaiah 53:5) Every spring we remember because of Easter that He indeed took our bruising, our crushing, and our punishment then He bore stripes so we could be healed and walk in newness of life! We get our new dresses and shoes and remember that He has given us new clothes to wear—a robe of righteousness and a crown of His glory, then sandals for our feet and rings for our fingers! We are His! We have new life because of His death on a cross and now we are raised to new life with Him! Spring—is an incredible time of year! It is the time of hope for a new future! Spring—new beginnings—we are new creatures—oh yes, spring!

Then comes summer! Summer times on the trail are wonderful there too. The water cools you from the summer heat, but when you are on the trail for a long time, you get quite hot! Even in the mountains, the summer can be hot! Here is Louisiana it is not unusual to have 98 degree days with 95 percent humidity! Heat index is about 110. During the summer you must make sure on these hikes that you take plenty of water. You can dehydrate quickly with the energy you exert hiking! Many times we would stop by a cascade, take our hiking boots off and place our feet in the water to cool off! Was it that the hike and the beauty changed? No it was the atmosphere that changed!

In the summer periods of our lives, it is our outlook that changes, the atmosphere of our hearts and minds. The infatuation with new life is now beginning to wane because of the heat and weariness of day to day activities. The beauty is still here—but it has now become work. It is no longer pleasant to go out and work in the flowerbeds and gardens. When we go out to work and pick the vegetables and fruit it is hot—we get thirsty and weary! It is like our strength is being tried to its limits! Fruit and vegetables are being produced and it is the time to work, persevere, have patience because this season will eventually end—endure to the end no matter what! It is a time that children are out of school. Family vacations take place where everyone is together for an extended period of time. Then they begin to get bored because it is hot, and there is no constructive daily activity and schedule—and they know they have to wait three months for school to start—so they are getting a bit hyper! They want to get in everything they can before getting down to the books again! Summer is a very important time in our lives as Christians. It is the season to plant and harvest the vegetables and taste the freshness of our labors. It is also a time we celebrate our Independence Day! As Christians we need to remember that once we become children of God, we declared our independence day from the kingdom of darkness! We are now children of light! We have reason to celebrate daily that Jesus translated us from darkness to light! Wow—we have a new citizenship in heaven. This is not my home, I am just passing through—but I am enjoying the ride while I am here on earth! We are now ambassadors in Christ! Wow! Summer—Independence Day for us!

Let's not forget the fall season! This is my most favorite season because it is the most beautiful! It is the time when everything is beginning to die and before the time of death it presents the best show ever! The leaves are red, orange, yellow, and greens—amazing! The colors show up in the mountains and it is one of the most visited times by many people! I can tell you being raised here in Louisiana there are very few color changes in the fall. But there in the mountains I was awe inspired by the colors of the leaves and wished I could bring home each tree!

Notice the things that were very important to give us breeze and shade in the summer months are no longer needed. These are the leaves! When their time of life is over, they display a wonderful profusion of color. Therefore God is His amazing wisdom knew that during this time the leaves needed to fall one at a time. In our lives when we are in that fall season, things fall out of our lives one at a time. Just imagine if God would allow a major storm to shake all the leaves at once! The small and weak trees would not survive the storm—therefore the Lord in His wisdom allows them to fall—slowly! Fall is a time to tear down and prepare for the winter months! I love the fact that right before the death of these leaves that blessed us so much in the summer breezes, they present their most amazing display before they fall away! Also remember that it is a time when we celebrate Thanksgiving! Thanksgiving for everything we are blessed with! Life, children, family, homes, eyes, hearts that beat properly, ears that hear, hands that can reach out and touch another soul, feet that can carry us around, voices that can sing, shout, and praise our God, emotions that allow us to "feel" joy, peace, love! We are so blessed and this time of fall is a wonderful time to remember how much we are blessed! We are saved, set free, our names are written in the Lamb's Book of Life! He has given us a chance for new life and filled us up with His Spirit! Oh how blessed we are—and how very thankful we should be!

Then we have the season of winter! Wow, winter—winter is necessary in our lives! As a matter of fact, if we did not have winters we would wear ourselves out! Winter is our time of resting and waiting on the Lord! Amazingly it is during the winter months when all the trees look dead and the plants look dead that the most life is taking place. If we could check into the center of the barks of the trees and down into the ground at the plants we would find that everything that those trees and plants need for an incredible spring to take place is happening during this winter season. During the resting and sitting at His feet is when we are getting everything we need to go forward when our springs rolls around. Do not try to hurry the winter time! Remember it is the time that we celebrate Christmas, the time of Jesus birth! It is the time we remember that God so loved the world—that is you too—that He gave His one and only Son that whoever believes in Him would not perish, but would have eternal life. (John 3:16) Winter—the time of rest and waiting on Him! Wow—how awesome!

You see, we are never just sitting through life. We are always going somewhere when we are His! Each season tells us that we are His and the fact that our seasons change tells us we are going forward! It is when our seasons do not change that we are in trouble! Remember:

Spring, Resurrection day and new birth
Summer, planting and harvesting, independence day
Fall, tearing down—thanksgiving
Winter, season of resting, enjoying the gift of Jesus

Remember dear friend, if God is for you, who can be against you? What can man do to you! Tremont Cascades remind me of all the seasons—and God is in the midst of them all—working them for our good and His incredible glory! Enjoy your seasons that change!

Chimney Tops

Chapter 8

Highlights: Views from the top to the mountain, big
trees
Hazards: Steep trail, ice in winter, pinnacles at top

*Now faith is being sure of what we hope for
and certain of what we do not see.
(Hebrews 11:1)*

Chimney Tops is a 4 mile roundtrip hike from
Newfound Gap Road. The trailhead starts 6.7
miles from Sugarland Visitors Center. Chimney Tops
is one of the most popular in the park because of
its length and spectacular views from the top of the
mountain. BUT, it is a steep uphill hike and can be
hazardous at the top. The rocky outcrops at the top
are steep, slippery when wet and exposed to wind and
lightening if it rains. To begin this hike you would

never suspect the steepness of the climb! There is a wonderful creek that runs through right at the beginning, and many an inspiring artist have come there to paint the scenes!

Like I said before, these people who write the hiking books are experts, so when they say a hike is a moderate one, you really need to think about this! Hmm—these guys are expert hikers, after all that's what they do— hike and write these books! Here we are lay people from the town of Walker, Louisiana. Can we do this one? This trail is two miles straight up to the top of the mountain! Needless to say, I have a struggle with a fear of heights! Amazing isn't it, and here I am hiking! OK—not so smart, but here we go! Like I said, at the beginning of the hike, the creek is so beautiful and amazing then you have the artist to watch too. It is not far past the creek that it turns into nothing but trail straight up the mountain!

I have to tell you, I am not a very good up the mountain person! Coming down is no problem, as a matter of fact most times I really love coming down! It is easy on you, no pressure, just go with the flow of gravity! Well, going up is going completely against the flow of gravity! It is absolutely amazing just how steep something can be! I found out on the "hike" of Chimney Tops that I would never want to be a mountain climber! Pure stupidity to me why a person would want to climb up a mountain!

You have to understand; I was born and raised in Louisiana. The biggest hill we have is the levee! My legs were not created to climb mountains, because I am convinced that God would have planted me in a mountain if they were! I am in great shape, do aerobics and keep up with my children and now grandchildren. But Chimney Tops will put the best to the test! As we read the manual, it said that there was an area that you would have to physically climb up and not just hike up. We were concerned about that part for the kids' sake, but then we thought, if it was really bad we would just come back down. Down I can handle. This mountain was so steep that before I knew it, I began to find myself leaning over to keep up with the steepness. Therefore, it was not only my legs burning, but my back took a toll in this too, especially with the backpack of food and drinks! There were frequent resting times on this hike—if you could of course find an area that was somewhat level. When we sat down, it was amazing just how quickly we would revive! Beef jerky does wonders at this stage of the hike! It replaces salt in the body that you lose in the hike—especially because the muscles are burning from the constant forward motion. Once my son decided to try walking backwards. At least that was using other muscles so the burning ones would stop burning for a bit! It worked OK, but there were serious drop offs and I told him, it is a long way down—no chance for survival! I thought about how when we are walking with God we become weary and tired from the fight. We need to find a level place to just sit and eat the Word of God to get the nourishment and rest we need.

Weariness crept in so many times because our thighs were burning like fire! The thing was, we were only about half way up. We could have given up then, or kept going! Just one mile more straight up, or start going down. Right at that time, a group came along and told us that the views at the top were incredible, and that unless you experience them, you could not describe them. They encouraged us to keep going! So we sat down to rest then started going forward! While resting, a chipmunk came running out of the forest and then ran straight up that trail like it was nothing! I was amazed! That little thing did not complain and it just moved forward! He saw the prize ahead — a big potato chip someone had dropped on the trail! He just ran toward his goal and took the prize! I realized that I needed to look at this hike in just that light! We were going ahead and boy was it going to be worth it! Are at least it better be!

Once we drank, snacked, caught our breath and rested, we were ready to move forward again! The scenery was beautiful. When we got over the steepness of the mountain and just rested, we were amazed at how beautiful it all was! Here we were in the middle of this amazing forest and we had not noticed it. We were all so overwhelmed by the climb itself that we were not paying attention to our surroundings! How many of us only see the trial we are in instead of realizing that there is so much around us that we need to stop and be thankful for. Amazingly once we sat down and rested, we were ready to go forward!

We came to a spot that was extremely rocky. Large rocks covered the trail and we had to climb over them. This was what we thought the book meant by spots of steep rocks and climbs! We looked at each other and said, "That wasn't so bad! That was really

weird. I guess they were trying to warn people!"
Then we continued on with the hike! Little did we
realize that those little rocks were not what they were
talking about! We were yet to see where you had to
climb hands and feet!

All at once I started to get really light headed and
dizzy! My children were beginning to get light headed
and dizzy too! Our wise leader, my husband, let us
know that we were experiencing altitude sickness.
We had to just sit and rest until our bodies adjusted to
the altitude! We were not used to breathing such thin
air! After all, in Louisiana we are below sea level—
here we were almost two miles above sea level. Just
a little bit of difference! Once we began to get our
heads together, we began to go forward again! My
husband picked at me and told me that I really was a
dizzy blonde! HAHAHAHAHAHA!

Up until this point we had not seen much of these
great views that we had heard about! It was very
obvious that there was a really long drop off, but
the forest hid the views from us. We knew that we
were almost there—because all the hikers coming
down would tell us—"You are almost there! Do not
give up—keep going—it's worth it! We promise—it
is well worth it!" OK, where is it??? I even heard a
couple of the kids say, I'm so sick of going up—I'm
ready to go down! I was with them, but I could not
tell them that! Two miles—boy, does that seemed
so long! Two whole miles—wow! On level ground
that is not so bad, but on this steep incline it felt like
four miles straight up! Just when I was about to open
my mouth and say, "That's it—I give up—I quit!

I've had enough of this uphill climb," an opening appeared and a huge tree appeared and a view that was incredible! But this was only half the view! To see the whole view you had to continue! Wow! It looked out at what seemed for miles and miles all you could see were the mountains! Birds were flying right by you—and you knew they were miles up from the road! This amazing tree was so big yet half of its roots were sticking out of the ground. Because it was on the south side of the mountain, it was protected from the fierce winds, so it was allowed to grow! What a majestic tree—you had to walk through the roots in order to continue on the trail! Then it showed up in my face! The rest of the "trail"! My husband was behind us so he took the picture when the four of us were going up. Straight up, at places on hands and knees—knowing there was nothing to catch you— the drop off was straight down two miles! Talk about using faith! I prayed like never before! Lord, help me now! Lord, help my children now—this crazy man is now taking us up here and we are at Your mercy! That's right, straight up! That would make the two miles up this mountain!

There are many times in our walk with the Lord that He ask us to just take steps of faith! We look at them and say, "Are you crazy! Surely you do not mean me! I can't do this! After all, I have a fear of heights. I am not used to mountain climbing; I do not think you would ever want me to feel uncomfortable! After all, You love me! And if You love me, You would never want me to do something I cannot!" Notice again, how many times we think of "I"—ouch!

Do you realize that God knows you better than you know you? He knows some of the fears that are holding you back and He also knows what you are capable of doing! After all He DID create you! Sometimes He allows us to be pushed a bit further than we think we can go just to show you that you can do it! Our heavenly Father does not want fear to be in our lives at all. All through the Bible, He constantly told people, to fear not, nor be dismayed for the Lord your God goes with you wherever you go! Do not be discouraged, do not be afraid—only take courage! Believe in God and you will succeed! Dear friend, God will make you come to a place of facing every one of your fears and all the things you think you cannot do, and He will show you that you can do ANYTHING through Him who gives you strength! Fear is there for one reason! To pull you back and push you back. To stop you dead in your tracks! I knew at this moment that if I did not go forward and face the fear of heights, that I would miss the views from the top of this mountain! I had great views where I stood, but just a bit further and the views would be amazing with nothing hindering my view! The key is completely placing our life and the lives of our children in His hands and trusting Him! Right up the face of the mountain was the goal I had started out for two miles down—I could not quit for my children, husband and for my God! Fear was not going to be my master! God is my master! Therefore, here we go!

This is one time that a picture just does not equal what we saw, it was spectacular! Wow, to think that God had created all of this! Once I got on top of that mountain, all I could see was the view! You could see as far as your eye would allow you too! It was a clear day and the light breeze on top of the mountain was so wonderful and then the birds all flying right above our heads! Wow! Here we were up in a bird's eye view! As I looked I realized that we could see so far, and cars looked so little to us up there, as a matter of fact, they were specks! The scripture in Isaiah 55:8 came to mind! *"For my thoughts are not your thoughts neither are your ways my ways,"* declares the LORD. *"As the heavens are higher than the earth, so are my ways higher than your ways and my thoughts than your thoughts."* I was getting just a glimpse of how God views things compared to the way we view things! He is so completely in control of all, and here we are peas in a valley and He is concerned for us! I looked at all the majesty of what He had created and considered for a moment— *Who am I that You are mindful of me and that You would care for me?* HE is God in heaven and here am I on earth—all I could do was just sit in awe and realize that I do not have a clue! I could live 900 years and would not even begin to grasp who God is to me and what on earth are we that He would consider us His children! Do you realize that He loves you? Yes YOU—right where you are! He knows you by name and He even knows how many days you are going to be here on earth! And in light of all this beauty we find in nature, who are we that He is mindful of us?

season to plant and harvest the vegetables and taste the freshness of our labors. It is also a time we cele- brate our Independence Day! As Christians we need to remember that once we become children of God, we declared our independence day from the kingdom of darkness! We are now children of light! We have reason to celebrate daily that Jesus translated us from darkness to light! Wow—we have a new citizenship in heaven. This is not my home, I am just passing through—but I am enjoying the ride while I am here on earth! We are now ambassadors in Christ! Wow! Summer—Independence Day for us!

Let's not forget the fall season! This is my most favorite season because it is the most beautiful! It is the time when everything is beginning to die and before the time of death it presents the best show ever! The leaves are red, orange, yellow, and greens—amazing! The colors show up in the moun- tains and it is one of the most visited times by many people! I can tell you being raised here in Louisiana there are very few color changes in the fall. But there in the mountains I was awe inspired by the colors of the leaves and wished I could bring home each tree! Notice the things that were very important to give us breeze and shade in the summer months are no longer needed. These are the leaves! When their time of life is over, they display a wonderful profusion of color. Therefore God is His amazing wisdom knew that during this time the leaves needed to fall one at a time. In our lives when we are in that fall season, things fall out of our lives one at a time. Just imagine if God would allow a major storm to shake all the tains, the summer can be hot! Here is Louisiana it is not unusual to have 98 degree days with 95 percent humidity! Heat index is about 110. During the summer you must make sure on these hikes that you take plenty of water. You can dehydrate quickly with the energy you exert hiking! Many times we would stop by a cascade, take our hiking boots off and place our feet in the water to cool off! Was it that the hike and the beauty changed? No it was the atmosphere that changed!

In the summer periods of our lives, it is our outlook that changes, the atmosphere of our hearts and minds. The infatuation with new life is now beginning to wane because of the heat and weariness of day to day activities. The beauty is still here—but it has now become work. It is no longer pleasant to go out and work in the flowerbeds and gardens. When we go out to work and pick the vegetables and fruit it is hot—we get thirsty and weary! It is like our strength is being tried to its limits! Fruit and vegetables are being produced and it is the time to work, persevere, have patience because this season will eventually end—endure to the end no matter what! It is a time that children are out of school. Family vacations take place where everyone is together for an extended period of time. Then they begin to get bored because it is hot, and there is no constructive daily activity and schedule—and they know they have to wait three months for school to start—so they are getting a bit hyper! They want to get in everything they can before getting down to the books again! Summer is a very important time in our lives as Christians. It is the

Who are we? We are His! We are the sheep of His pasture—His prized possession that He loved enough to leave the throne of Heaven and come down to walk this earth so that we would be drawn to Him! Oh, just sit and think how much He loves you!

What was really funny to me was the fact that on top of that mountain where the winds I am sure can become extremely fierce, and not much but rock and weird bushes exist there appeared a little squirrel! This little one was not afraid or anything or anyone! He was very happy being a thief! You would set your potato chips or cookies and crackers down and he would be very happy to come and snatch them up. I thought of the parable that Jesus told us in the Bible about not to worry—"Look at the birds of the air; they neither toil nor sow, or reap or store away in barns, and yet your heavenly Father feeds them. Are you not much more valuable than they?" (Matthew 6:26) Well this little squirrel was being fed by our heavenly Father through all us crazies that would make this 2 mile hike up this mountain! He was fat, and he was also hiding all the goodies in a cave on top of that mountain for the winter! Even this little squirrel here on the top of this mountain is being taken care of by our Father—through us!

Now for our trip down the mountain! I never thought about coming down! Going up on this steep end was a whole lot easier than going down! Going up kept your eyes up, now coming down; we suddenly had to see the drop off! This was not good! I informed my husband that he got us up that mountain, now he was going to be the first down and help the rest of us down! As long as we focused on the drop off, we were in trouble because fear once again began to grip us. But when we got our eyes focused on one step at a time, we were able to do it! I prayed like never before—then I remembered when Elijah prayed that God would open his servant's eyes and show him that God had angels to protect them, and I remembered that we had angels stationed around us! I was just not sure if they were responsible for crazies like us who purposely climbed up there! Finally we all made it back to the huge tree and rested there again. We all talked about the view on top of that mountain—it was the best view we had ever seen! And that squirrel just amazed all of us! My son asked a question I remember so well. He asked me why the squirrel stayed up there, when there was all this food down here on the trail. The trail was not far from where he was, but he never traveled down and realized this!

I began to realize just how many of us are right at the brink of something incredible God has for us, but because we do not leave our comfort zone—the place where we feel secure, even though it was quite dangerous, we can miss it! There we are struggling and striving trying to make it. All along God could be saying, "Just take a step of faith, and I'll have something so much better for you if you would just believe!"

We took some friends "hiking" at Tunica Hills in Mississippi/Louisiana border, just some little hills. All of us began to climb up this hill to get to the next waterfall. One girl started to climb and was giving up just about one foot from the top of the hill. I began telling her, "Do not dare give up, you are almost here—just one more step and you will have it! You can do it—do not give up!" Well, she made it, but I know many in the Christian walk that do that same thing! When the going gets a bit too tough, they quit—not necessarily leaving the Christian walk, but that is where they stop! If they would just take a few more steps, they would be at the destiny God has for them. Remember, we go from glory to glory! That is, one mountain to the next!

Now for the trip down! We were all excited—yeah! We are going down now—this was going to be easy—right? After all, we were now going with gravity, not against it! Well, after about a mile down, the other parts of our legs started hurting because of the steepness of the downhill climb! Actually I don't know which was worst! There were rocks and leaves that made the trail slippery, so we had to pay close attention to every step. Then the steepness of the mountain was another hurdle! OK, downhill wasn't so wonderful either! We stopped often, because we needed to rest our minds from watching every step—then we again realized how wonderful our surroundings! The sights downhill were so beautiful, we could look down and begin to see the creek far away—but you also saw a trail of wildflowers going down. We were too busy looking up to notice what was right there on the way up. It wasn't until we began to just take it slow, rest and look around that we embraced all of our surroundings! In our walk with the Lord, let's not get so busy focused on one thing that we fail to notice all the little blessings God places all around us to enjoy! You know— things like food on the table, friends, family, homes we live in, birds, squirrels, trees, flowers, jobs, church building and our pastor and leaders. The list can go on and on—we are so blessed here in this country, yet we do not realize it! Unfortunately, we get caught up in the give-me-more mentality or I need this or that instead of thanking God for what we already have right here in our laps!

We made it down that mountain, it was a challenge, and a few years later we did it again! All of us said how we forgot the steepness and the length of that trail, but you know what, the views were still amazing and the scenery incredible! The trail did not change, we did! We enjoyed it so much the second time and we were able to encourage everyone who decided to try that trail!

Do not be afraid to try something amazing and different that will cause your faith in God to grow! May He never say I asked you to do this and I wouldn't because I was afraid! He is worthy of my trust—and I say, let's go for it! Your victory could be just around the bend! Do not stop, do not give up—keep going forward, one step at a time!

Trust in the Lord with all your heart and lean not on your own understanding; in all your ways acknowledge Him, and He shall direct your paths. Pro 3:5-6

Mama and Daddy Intermission

Chapter 9

Even though I walk through the valley of the shadow of death, I will fear no evil, for you are with me; your rod and your staff they comfort me. (Psalm 23:4)

Before we go on to the next adventure, I wanted to take a little time and share with you the beauty and bitter sweetness of life! Everything in our lives is there for a purpose. Nothing happens by accident—it's all for a purpose of making us more in the image of our Maker and Savior the Lord Jesus Christ! Recently in my life there have been some major events that were bitter and yet at the same time very sweet! My mama had been sick for several years, but in the last three years she had taken a turn for the worst! She had rheumatoid arthritis, breast cancer, she had a stint placed in her heart and the bones of her spine were deteriorating. In order to survive the pain she lived with, a pain pump was installed inside of her. She had always been a very active person and she loved gardening! When I grew up, I always remember my mama lovingly sewing all of us clothes! Store bought items were just not good enough—she lovingly made them with her hands for her children. I remember gardening and shucking corn, pealing purple hull peas, snapping beans— we had to freshest vegetables ever. Many of the talents I have today I realize now came from my mama. My love of flowers, floral arranging, baking breads, cooking, sewing and my love for music—talents that the Lord saw fit to pass down from my mama to me. From my daddy came the love of teaching, art, love for people and the great gift of gab! Father God placed my mama and daddy together to create who I have become. Now everything I do for the kingdom of God goes to my mama and daddy's credit too.

My daddy was always there and they knew what hard work was all about! My daddy was a school teacher—a task that is so important to all of our futures! Teachers mold and help create each student's personality! Many people remember my daddy as one who helped them so much! He was always the strong one of our family, and I never saw my daddy fall apart! He unselfishly gave up much in order to provide for his family. Pinching pennies was part of life and they did it so well. We were not rich and as children, we had to get jobs to save for some of the things we desired to have. Mama and Daddy were not "bless me" people—they were the ones who taught us the value of money and things. Today I see so many people giving their children everything on a silver platter because they feel guilty—but unfortunately they have created a "me" generation that only thinks about themselves. Mama and Daddy loved us too much for that!

Unfortunately, it was many years later that I finally realized all the good my mama and daddy did for me! Because of this there were many lost years that in the end, God made up for! In all the years my mama was sick, my daddy was right there—he never gave up but held on to the love he had for my mama and the trust he had in God. When she died, they were married 61 years! The last few days of my mama's life were very hard days and our family passed the test and came together! Through those last days God taught me so much and I pass this onto you!

It was a week and a half of very bitter-sweet times. The sweet—my mama knew this was it. She told us all goodbye, and each one of us were able to tell her just how much we loved her and that we were going to take care of Daddy! On her dying bed, she was still concerned for my daddy! During that time, my mama apologized for not loving me like I needed to be loved! It was then that God gave me such an incredible revelation! My mama and daddy were the perfect parents for me! They were exactly what I needed for me to become the person God intended me to be for the call He had on my life! No one else on this planet could have been better parents to me than these precious souls of my dearest Mama and Daddy! Even the sister and brother I had were all of God's design. He knows from the beginning to the end and everything in between. We cannot in any way understand His plan, but we must learn to embrace it, and hold on to it, even if it means releasing someone we dearly love into His loving nail scarred hands. The sweetness was that once I passed through the cross, all the bitter from the pass was made sweet! HE was about to create a new thing—a freshness and cleanness that could only come through the trials, tribulations, joys, and heartaches that He had allowed! I am so grateful for the choice of my Heavenly Father for who my mama and daddy were going to be! As I look back, I remember all the sacrifices, the heartaches, the fun times, even some of those times I thought then, were so hard! Those are the true gifts that no one can ever take from me. The only price tag it came with was the self-sacrifice of my mama and daddy for our family! They did the best they knew how, and that was more than enough! These are the principles that they taught us about what is really important in life—time with each other, sharing our gifts and talents with others and teaching others what is important in life. Success in life is not about a thing; things all wear out and pass away! It is not about a person; no one came make you happy or sad, that is your choice. It is not about your accomplishments or what position you achieve in life; it's not about how great you are or how much money you have; it's not about how many friends you have, ministries you are involved in or how much you do in your church!

Bottom line like Solomon says in Ecclesiastes 12:13-14 (NAS)

The conclusion when all has been heard is: fear God and keep His commandments, because this applies to every person. For God will bring every act to judgment, everything which is hidden weather it is good or evil.

As we watched my mama in those last days of her life, the only thing that mattered to me was that this was MY MAMA, and I had to release her into the hands of a loving God! No matter how much I KNEW she was going to be better off with Jesus, my heart did not want to let her go! This was the bitter and I wanted to be strong for my daddy who had been strong for me so many times. In those last days my mama's body was shutting down! While she was conscience, she told the doctors, "Do not keep me alive, let me go!" She took that burden off of us all—none of us had to make that decision. During those last days, all of her children and most of her grandchildren were able to tell her goodbye! She very graciously and lovingly told us all goodbye and that she loved us! As a loving Mama and grandmother, and great-grandmother, she made her peace with all of us and left us all realizing that we would greatly desire to do the same when our time came! Though we would sorely miss her, we knew we did not want her to continue "living" here on earth in the pain she suffered. You see, she was no longer living, she only existed! My daughter told me one day after seeing her grandmother struggling to breathe, "Mama, could they just give her a drug overdose?" I reminded her of Psalm 139:16(NAS):

> Your eyes have seen my unformed substance;
> And in Your book were all written, the days
> that were ordained for me, when as yet there
> was not one of them.

All of our days were written in His book before we were even here. God knew the last day my mama was going to be here on this earth and we had to trust His plan. Those days were hard, watching my mama's body draw closer and closer to death, hearing the death rattle as she breathed and seeing her body of death holding on. Then watching the heartache of my daddy losing his life's love, we prayed for God's mercy. Yet once they were finally over, all of us breathed a sigh of relief and then of heartache knowing that her life was over. Then it hit me—everything I do, every word I write, every song I sing, every picture I take and every message I preach is not only for God's glory, but also an extension of who my mama and my daddy are to me! That is the sweet!

When life gives us lemons to deal with, if we take them to our Heavenly Father, He will throw in the cross and the cross will make it all sweet. Then He will give it back to us so we will have sweetened lemonade. The amazing thing about lemonade is that it is a diuretic. It helps to remove the impurities out of our systems and any water retention that can be harmful in our bodies. When I came to the Lord on

April 18, 1990, I had no idea that God was about to place the wood of the cross in every bitter situation in my life and make every one sweet! But I am here to tell you—He did and He is willing to do it for you!

I appreciate and cherish the gift of my mama and daddy in my life. Today, dear friend, sit back and realize that everything that has happened in your life is a gift from God if you will only allow Him to make every bitter moment sweet! Sit back, pour yourself a big glass of lemonade, and realize that the drink you are enjoying first started with bitter lemons! It is the sweetness that makes it enjoyable—our sweetness is His cross!

Today, call your Mama and Daddy and tell them just how much you love them and appreciate everything they have done in your life! If you have a broken relationship with them, just wait, because God will make it beautiful in His timing! They are a joy and your gift from the Lord, what you do with your life is their joy and your gift back to them and the Lord! Remember one of the 10 commandments was Honor your mother and father! It is the first commandment with a promise, that you may have long life!

Thank you Father for the gift of my mama and daddy—bless them today. I know my mama is in Heaven right now, and I know that Jesus is showing her the beautiful flower garden He has planted for her to enjoy. The seeds from her garden came from all the unselfish things she did for our lives! Rejoice Mama, because as Psalm 23 says:

The Lord is my Shepherd I shall not want...
And I will dwell in the house of the Lord,
forever and ever and ever!

For Mama—I love you!
Mary Essel Ducote February 1, 1926 -
August 7, 2007

Cades Cove

Chapter 10

*Keep your lives free from the love of money
and be content with what you have, because
God has said, "Never will I leave you; never
will I forsake you." (Hebrews 13:5)*

Cades Cove is a wonderful valley that is
completely surrounded by majestic mountains.
When you walk or drive through the cove area you
get a sense and feel for the people who once lived
there. It is a magical place filled with the wonder
of nature itself. You cannot go through the cove
without realizing how God had indeed smiled down
on that little area. It is filled with creeks, waterfalls, deer, foxes, beautiful forest, wonderful hiking
trails, horses and pasture lands. Each time you turn
around you are staring at a new beauty that only God
created! I cannot imagine the bravery of the people

who lived there. Their character had to be like some of the original settlers, pioneers willing to brave the unknown in order to find a place to raise family. They went to a place that was unknown that could be filled with many dangers and chose to settle there. With every new beginning there are mixed emotions of fear, excitement, expectation and complete trust in the Lord that even though you make a bad decision, God is still well able to turn it around for your good and His glory. These are the true heroes! They risked life and limb to live life for the good of their family, their fellow man and for the glory of God.

In the midst of the cove are three churches. Once these pioneers built their own homes, they built the church building. It was a place that they could gather together to worship God and see to their neighbors needs. They truly lived the life of God first, family then their fellow neighbors.

Today our focus has changed because our world around us changes so fast! We have to be careful that our focus is not trying to keep up with the Jones's, but our focus should be just as theirs was. Their focus was not on what was outdated or how they needed to change their surroundings to "make themselves feel better" or to keep up with the changing times. Their focus was on surviving and being thankful for what they did have.

On one of our trips to Cades Cove we were blessed to have one of the last "teachers" of the school in the Cove. This lady was in her 90s and yet still had all her wits about her. Two of my "A" students got up to do the spelling bee as it was done back then. We were all amazed at how this 90-year-old was able to get the best out of all the kids! It was exciting to sit there and watch this wonderful lady do her work! This little old lady stumped all the kids that were there—who says we are so much smarter now?

Amazingly, when we look back at the past, suicides were unheard of. People were content with what they had and thankful for every day they lived. Cades Cove brings that home as you walk through the trails, the graveyards and take a look at the homes in which they lived! They had a school and churches—and their faith in the Lord. These people were surrounded with the fact that God was indeed with them. All they had to do was step outside and see the majestic mountains and the valley in which they lived. Life was hard, but they realized that life itself was a gift from God. Every breath they took was evidence that God did indeed exist and that he had a plan for them. As long as they were here on earth—they KNEW the plan God had for them was not finished. Once life was over, grief and mourning was there, but also they rejoiced that their loved ones was going home to be with Jesus. There was no time to even consider how "bad" they had it or how depressed they were. They were too busy staying alive and being thankful! Have you realized that if you concentrate on what you have to be thankful for, you would not have much time to consider all the big, bad and ugly of this life? When things are rough, normally if we wait around long enough, they do tend to change.

As I walked around the cove it was not hard to see that they had it **very** hard. Working the land was not as easy as climbing on a tractor or going to Home Depot or Wal-mart to get what they needed. In order to build their homes and barns and churches, they had to cut down their own trees and prepare them to build these buildings with their own hands. They knew that home was not a building, and church not a building—they KNEW that home and church were in their own hearts. They knew that the buildings were only shelter, and what they passed down to their children was a deep abiding love for each other and God. Everything they needed was there in the cove, and in order to get it they had to work for it. Nothing was handed to them and everyone had a job to do, from the youngest to the oldest. Everyone was needed!

Today I see so many people looking for "their" place in this world. So many are looking for where they fit. Have our families failed so badly? Funny how back then you knew you were needed and people were counting on you. How sad today that we have forgotten those great truths! Each of us has something to give. If we just look past our own desires, wants and dreams, instead of what we do not have or what we want and begin to look at what our family, neighbors, friends, and churches needs, we would be more content with life. Too many of us have allowed our lives to become dots, the dots being ourselves with the whole world rotating around us. The precious souls of bygone days did not have that luxury.

At the same time that I began thinking about this chapter, I was reading the book of Ecclesiastes in the

Bible. The thoughts of Solomon are so true. Solomon was a man who was rich, had many wives and concubines; he was so wise that people came from far away just to hear him speak, he had accomplished everything possible in his life then suddenly he realized that it was all just a chasing after the wind. As I thought about this and considered those in the Cades Cove area, I realized that we are walking so far away from what it's all about, and then we wonder why we are not satisfied and happy in life.

I have to confess, my favorite show up to this point was HGTV. My husband lovingly calls it "Covet TV." But at the same time, my husband's favorite TV show is sports, sports and more sports. I call it "Idol TV". Did you notice how both of these TV shows are all about how much better we can make our world and how winning depends on other people? It was at that time I began to notice just how much the HGTV shows talked about updating "everything" because it was now old. I am not saying changing things is wrong, but when we begin to change things in order to make us feel better or just because we feel what we have are outdated even though it still works—that is when we get into a trap. You see, we are the only persons who can make us happy and that is only by knowing and realizing just how blessed we actually are. Changing my world will not take away my problems or make them feel better, changing my attitudes and thought life about them certainly will. As I said before, it is amazing that there was no talk about suicides back in the Cades Cove days. People were not successful because they had accomplished so much or because they had the "right" job, or the perfect wife/ husband or because they had everything they wanted. They were successful because they were alive, had a relationship with God and their families and friends to share any extras with! They were not puffed up with pride because they knew they could have a time when they would need neighbors too. These people knew what it was to sow and reap.

I hear all the time, *"If my husband will just talk with me more, if my wife would desire me more, if I had a better job, if I had this or that or this would happen and that would happen"* — always looking somewhere else.

As we look at Solomon we see someone who had it all — and he still was not happy. At the end of his life his conclusions about life were fear God and keep His commandments. I love the book of Ecclesiastes. At the beginning of Solomon's kingly reign his prayer was for God to give him wisdom to rule His people. You have to remember first off where Solomon came from. He was David's son. His mother was the woman that David sinned with then his dad had Solomon mother's first husband killed. Imagine if you will how his "brothers and sisters" felt about him. He also grew up watching all the wickedness of David's other sons. Amnon devised a scheme so he could rape his half sister, Absalom killed Amnon, and anarchy reigned as a part of Solomon's life. He ran with his father, David, from his brother Absalom and came back after Absalom was killed by the armies of David. Solomon also watched as his father mourned the deaths of his sons realizing that his sin was part of the curse that was happening to his family. Simple family life was completely unknown to our dear Solomon. I feel because of the way he grew up that he may have chased after everything that this world could give to make him happy. God blessed Solomon not only with wisdom to rule the people, but because he did not ask for "things" God blessed him with everything he could imagine. Then he finally realized that nothing of this world would satisfy him.

Ecclesiastes 2:10-11(NIV) says:

> I denied myself nothing my eyes desired; I refused my heart no pleasure, my heart took delight in all my work, and this was the reward for my labor. Yet when I surveyed all that my hands had done and what I had toiled to achieve, everything was meaningless, a chasing after the wind; nothing was gained under the sun. Still Solomon was not happy or satisfied.

Things or accomplishments will never replace what we can only get from a relationship with Jesus. I remember before the Lord called me that I thought if I could just go to college or if I could just get this type of job, or if this child would just behave or if this or if that—chasing after the wind. Bottom line was that once I called on the name of the Lord Jesus to be my Savior and Lord, and then submitted my life to Him alone, my life finally began. Just like the people in Cades Cove, the only thing that mattered was that "Jesus loved me, this I know, for the Bible tells me so." Life was not all peaches and cream as I grew up, many hard things happened in my life and I could not imagine them ever becoming anything beautiful or even working for my good and our Lord God's glory—but they have.

A pearl is formed because a grain of sand comes into the oyster and begins to irritate it. In order to stop the irritation the oyster begins to excrete a fluid that produces a pearl. I now realized that each time I have allowed the blood of Jesus to cover over the "grains of sand" in my life a new pure pearl was formed. Then when my life is over Jesus will step up to me and hand me a string of pearls that was created only because of the trials, tribulations and sorrows I have walked through. These are the things that the people in Cades Cove realized. It was what Solomon finally began to realize. God does make all things beautiful in their time. He does it so that men will revere Him. What God does no one can add to it or take away from it, God makes it perfect!

This life is such a short time and what we do here will determine our eternity. The people at Cades Cove were willing to brave whatever elements in order to serve God, family and community. Life was so simple yet so rewarding. It was so hard yet gave them reason to be alive. As I visit Cades Cove I think on the simple yet hard life it was there. I can just imagine neighbors during harvest time sharing work with each other. Just imagine Thanksgiving celebration there with family, friends thanking God for every morsel they eat and for the fact that they are still alive. How great our lives would be if we would just remember those days of old in a time that was hard, yet so blessed.

As I sit for just a second and think of the blessing I have I become overwhelmed. I can breathe on my own, I do not need a machine; I can walk, talk, sit, and stand all on my own. Each morning when I awake I look out and SEE the beauty of the new day and HEAR the birds singing in the day of the Lord. I have a roof over my head, clothes on my back and many more in a closet and drawers, I have food to eat, a stove to cook on and a car that gets me to and from work. I have a job and many precious people God has placed in my life to help guide me and encourage me in my walk with Him and many that He allows me to encourage and touch for Him. Family, friends, church, flowers surrounding my yard and tall and majestic trees in our yard! My body functions each day and I am alive to share the love of Jesus with others. I have a machine that plays music and a piano that I play to praise the name of my Lord. I have wonderful neighbors who love me and whom I love. I have a husband who loves me—a father who loves me and needs me. Wow—notice none of the things I mentioned has to do with anything being updated! Many of them are old, getting worn, but oh so special! My prayer is that on that day when I go home to Heaven and see my Jesus that I will hear, "Well done my good and faithful servant!" The important thing is not being the most noticeable to man—it is being one noticed by God!

A long time ago I desired to be up on a pulpit preaching and sharing the Word and seeing many saved! An evangelist of the evangelists! My desire now is but to be a door keeper in my Heavenly Father's house gazing upon His beauty on a daily basis! I believe that the people—the settlers—pioneers of Cades Cove—daily as they woke up each morning were given the gift of being door keepers here on earth and gazing at our Father's beauty each morning as they looked at the mountains, valleys, waterfalls, flowers, deer, horses and the beautiful sun rise! The simple things in life—those are what will last forever! This appreciation is what I desire to pass down not only to my children and grandchildren, but also with every person I come in contact with! Our Heavenly Father loves a heart of thanksgiving! Dear one, look around you—just begin to count your blessings; count them one by one and see what your beautiful Heavenly Father has done!

Each time I go to Cades Cove, I remember these lessons—God, family, neighbors—it is the order that God has created for us! Then I remember the Sabbath day, keeping it holy before the Lord! The Sabbath day is the day we stop to take notice of the blessings of God in our lives! I am ashamed to say that I have not done that enough! But praise the Lord that His wonderful mercies are new every morning and His incredible loving-kindness reaches to the skies! As we praise and give thanksgiving before our Lord, look up, because we know His wonderful Word that tells us He is right there rejoicing over us!

Trust in the LORD, and do good;
Dwell in the land and feed on His faithfulness.
Delight yourself in the LORD
And He will give you the desires of your heart!
Commit your way to the LORD
Trust also in Him,
And He shall bring it to pass.
He shall bring forth your righteousness as the
   light,
And your justice as the noonday.
Rest in the LORD and wait patiently for Him...
   Psalm 37:3-7a (NKJV)

Roan Mountain

Chapter 11

Highlights: Cloudland, Balds, Scenic overlooks and
            Rhododendron Gardens
Hazards: Rocky trails
Connects with the Appalachian Trail

*Find rest, O my soul, in God alone; my hope
comes from him. He alone is my rock and
my salvation; he is my fortress, I will not be
shaken. (Psalms 62:5-6)*

What a wonderful place Roan Mountain is!
God's hand designed a special feature for
His children of the Pisgah National Forest of North
Carolina and Cherokee National Forest of Tennessee.
Roan Mountain is 6,285 foot ridge straddling the
North Carolina and Tennessee state lines. Our chil-
dren loved to stand on the state line and place one

foot in North Carolina and the other in Tennessee. This brought them great delight to be in two states at the same time! The mountain has beautiful gardens of magenta blossom rhododendrons. Treeless areas called "balds" that offer panoramic views across a sweeping flow of grasses, spruce-fir forest and the site of the Cloudland Hotel. Its name is linked to many legends. One legend says Daniel Boone was a frequent mountain visitor, riding his "roan" or reddish-colored horse—hence the name. Another legend says that it got its name from the thickets of rhododendron gardens with their thousands of pink and lavender blossoms in late June.

This state park does not take reservations; it is a first come first serve basis. Therefore, we would have to leave our home in Walker, Louisiana at around 4:00 P.M. Then we would drive all night so we could arrive at the gates of Roan Mountain State Park prayerfully at around 7:30 A.M. the next morning. The drive there was the worst part of the trip. In order to stay awake, my husband and I would drink an overabundance of coffee. As you can imagine, we would be a nervous wreck by the time we did got there. To my amazement I always manage to have my turn at driving around 2:00 A.M.

The children would be excited about going to Roan Mountain, but around 12:00 A.M. they would finally crash—many times the crash was a very loud one before silence would occur! One of the times on our way to the Roan, I was driving and everyone asleep. It was very late and in order to stay awake I had the music turned up and I was singing and praising the Lord. No one in the vehicle minded because they were all asleep. After some time, I began to really get sleepy. I started praying for the Lord to speak to me or something to keep me awake! Suddenly I noticed a terrible smell and it was coming from outside! It was so bad that it made me nauseated! Looking around I realized that in the middle of this nasty smell were homes and office buildings. I was perplexed that people could live in the midst of that horrible smell. All the kids and my husband sleeping in the van were unaware of the smell. Suddenly I heard the Lord say, "Child, so many people live just like this. They have been living in stench for so long that they have become used to it. But, I am going to send you to different places as a breath of fresh air—so that when they smell the fragrance that I will give you they will remember what freshness of life can be!"

Many times when the Lord speaks to us we do not understand what He is really saying to us. At the time I did not understand what He was trying to tell me. Oh I did have my delusions of grandeur—but they were just that delusions. It was not until many years later that God opened my eyes to realize what He was trying to tell me. So many people are living under the stench of condemnation and guilt and they truly do not know what freedom is! I was one of those people. The stench of my own imperfections and my own inability to make people happy filled me with guilt and condemnation. I felt like a failure because I could not be what people wanted me to be. This held me in a prison of constantly feeling guilty and condemned. Prison ministry is one of the things that I love to do.

Prisoners are just people like us who made wrong choices and now they are paying for those choices. In order to go to prison, you must appear before a judge and then the judge sentences you in respect to the crime you have committed. That is what condemnation and guilt are like. Being sentenced for a crime you have done, yet you never get set free. For every new mistake, you are condemned for more time to serve. Our judges are the people around us—it can be our parents, friends, leaders at our church, family, friends and anyone around us. When we walk in condemnation and guilt, we have not yet been able to receive the grace of God through Christ Jesus. Scripture says in Ephesians 2:8-9 (NKJ), "For by grace you have been saved through faith; and that not of yourselves, it is a gift of God; not of works lest anyone should boast." It is never by works—what we do, how perfectly we do it, or whom we please. Our works are only temporary. Once we make a mistake or disappoint someone, we are a failure once again. But grace—GRACE is forever and a gift of God.

One of my favorite praise songs is Amazing Grace—the old version and the new. Somehow I could teach about grace, even knew that the definition of grace was *God's Redemption At Christ's Expense*, yet I could not receive it for myself. I knew in my mind that when Jesus laid his life down on that cross for me that His blood flowed down so that my rap sheet would be covered and wiped clean. I could tell you that my rap sheet, covered with all the fears and failures,—was under the blood of Jesus! But still something was holding me in that prison—

and I began to wonder if I would ever be set free. In order to fully be covered in His grace I had to first believe that it was for me too and then I had to receive His unmerited grace. Some time the problem is that our receiver is broken! I could give, actually I loved giving and serving, but receiving was an issue. I grew up believing that I had to earn everything. Receiving gifts was something foreign to me. Even when I received a gift, constantly I was reminded what I had been given and how I owed ___ for it! This mindset had to be broken—and if you think about something breaking a crash normally occurs. Well, God did bring me to that crash! Slowly I began to be able to receive from people, but it made me very uncomfortable—it was so much easier to give! In giving there was no threat, but when I received, in my warped mind of condemnation, it would put me in debt to that person—a debt that I would never be able to repay. When I grew up, I carried that guilt and condemnation from everyone around me.

When my mama was not happy, it was my fault, when something went wrong, it was my fault—if we had financial problems, it was my fault because I was sick. I was stuck in a prison that was more real than the physical prisons that I go into. Roman's 8:1 says: "There is now no condemnation for those who are in Christ Jesus for the law of the Spirit of life in Christ Jesus has set you free from the law of sin and death." Then verse 15 of that same chapter in the New American Standard Version says: "For you have not received a spirit of slavery leading to fear again, but you have received a spirit of adoption as sons by which we cry out, Abba Father." "It is for freedom that Christ has set us free; therefore do not let yourselves be burdened again by a yoke of slavery." (Galatians 5:1) What is that "yoke of slavery?" I believe that it is fear—fear of condemnation and guilt—fear of being in the wrong! Fear is not from God—God does not give us a spirit of fear, but of power, love and a sound mind (see 2 Timothy 1:7). Actually perfect love casts out all fear (see 1 John 4:18) Who is perfect love? God! I knew all the right scriptures, why could I not walk in them?

Grace—grace is something Roan Mountain taught me so much about! Grace is a gift—it cannot be bought nor can it be earned! It is a gift that God chooses to just pour out on you. This is how God began to show me about grace.

OK, we have driven all night, everybody is on everybody else's nerves and tempers are flaring! No sleep, too much caffeine, too much sugar and it equals a very serious situation. Dynamite has nothing on this! Now what you have to remember is that once we get there, then we wait for the gate to open, prayerfully get a campsite, then comes the setup. Our setup involved the five of us setting up two tents and one cooking screened tent. Then we had to blow up four mattresses, one queen size and three twins. Being a very organized person, I had a plan set up for each child and for my husband and myself. We had to unload the van, get the tent sites ready and then prepare to set the tents up. The children knew that before they could go explore and play, all tents, mattresses, the kitchen and luggage had to be set up—then they could go have all the fun they wanted. Each of us had a job to do and once we got everyone moving on their jobs, it did not take long for all areas to be completed. On this particular time, we had a campsite right next to the stream. The water was so incredible, and the melody of the stream called us to come, stop, sit and rest! Stop all the activity and come!

Once everything was set up, everyone went check out the campground. It was then that I was left alone for a while, and it was like God had planned this time for me and Him! It seemed that everyone got the message and left: even those camping by us were gone! I was completely alone. As I started walking toward the stream of running water I spotted a large rock basked by the sun. A very large tree was right next to it and it made a perfect back rest. Sitting on that rock with my back on the tree, suddenly all the tension began to ease away! The sun with its warmth was just what I needed. As I dangled a hand in the water of the stream I could sense the presence of Almighty God! There I was tired, stressed, weary with a great desire to just fall apart! Loss of sleep has a tendency to do that to you—but in the middle of this chaos God appears! He began to show me that just as I was seated on the rock, in the Spirit I was also seated on the Rock Christ Jesus no matter how much I felt I had failed. As I leaned on the tree, in the Spirit the cross was always there for me to lean on and remember the price paid for me and the invitation it gave to me so that I could come to Him! Just as the sun shone down around me and warmed me, so in the Spirit the Son of God shines down on me and warms me with His blanket of love. Just as my hand sat in the water of the stream, so the water of His word washes me clean. This is grace—it is nothing we have done or could ever do—He receives us in spite of our imperfections and failures, and He desires for us to lean on Him! In and of ourselves we are nothing but failures and full of imperfections. But as we sit with Him being refreshed by His great love for us,—it is then that we realize that we cannot fail! "If God is for us, then who can be against us?" (Roman's 8:31 NIV) What can man do to us?

Before I knew it, I was sound asleep engulfed in His awesome presence. The melody of that stream lulled me to sleep and rest. It was the very thing that this poor body, soul and spirit needed after such a long, tiring trip. In life there are many long tiring trips we take. Some of them are our jobs, our children, relationships, ministry even our own emotions—but the answer for each is the same—basking in His loving tenderness. Ephesians is one of my favorite books of the Bible—and I love that in the first chapter in the New King James version "kind intentions" is mentioned three times. The kind intentions of the Lord our God—I had to realize that He does have kind intentions toward me. No matter what I have been through in life the answer is the same—Him—time spent with Him!

In His presence are blessings ever more. In His presence is healing, deliverance, security, love, joy, peace, tenderness and peace! There is not another place in this world that we can go to get what we

118

need except from Him! No thing or man will be able to give it to us.

The amazing thing about Roan Mountain State Park is that it is not unusual to wake up in the morning and see someone in their morning walk praying or sitting on the picnic table reading the Word of God. It was the most amazing thing I had ever experienced. The whole park was there for families to enjoy time together and God's beautiful creation. There is a peaceful flowing steam running through the park that is stunning. Our kids' loved to tube down the stream; we were able to sit and rest at the stream—if we happened to get in a reclining position, it would not be long before we were asleep by the stream. It was completely different from all the other places we had gone. The whole place was filled with the peace of God!

There was a little Baptist church that came up each Sunday and held services for the people there and they had one thing in mind. Feed the sheep of God physically and spiritually! The people there were not in the height of fashion—actually most of their clothes were homemade and plain—just good old country folks! It was as if God in His grace and mercy made this place just so people could come and rest and get refreshed in Him! Those folks who lived there were there just to serve! That is God's whole place for the body of Christ!

When you wanted to go hiking, all you had to do was drive up to the top of the mountain and there was all the hiking you wanted to do. The Appalachian Trail is connected right up in the middle of the

Rhododendron Gardens. It is shocking that you can leave the campground in shorts, and then when you get to the top of the mountain and the trails,—the temperature drops around 20 to 30 degrees.

The gardens are beautiful in the middle of the summer and the forest of spruce trees wonderful! There was an amazing overlook that was spectacular! You could see for miles the beauty of the mountains' terrain. On one of the hikes you drive up to the "balds" and start hiking. It was the first hike that I found going down was worst than going up. The rocks on the trail made it dangerous going down and the trails were very narrow. They were unlike any we had gone on before.

One of the hiking trails leads to the site of where the old Cloudland Hotel sat. In 1885, Civil War General John T. Wilder built a 300-room hotel on top of Roan Mountain. Cloudland Hotel became a retreat for hay fever sufferers and for the city folk. One ad stated, "Come up out of the sultry plains to the Land of the Sky—magnificent views where the rivers are born. There are over 100 mountaintops over 4,000 feet high in sight. Around 1910 the building was abandoned. What attributed to the hotel's destruction were the expense of shipping goods and the very short three month business season. When we went to see the site where the hotel was, we were walking in the clouds. It was incredible to feel the clouds move across the mountaintop, realizing that we were standing in the midst of the clouds! WOW!! The children loved it! Walking with the clouds! It was there that you realized why God had indeed visited that area in a special way! You could go into the valley and sit by the streams or go up to the clouds and walk there with God!

It made me think of Enoch—how he just walked with God. He was then he was not—God just took him. It is my desire in my life to walk that closely with the Lord!

I had a special Jewish friend that passed away from ALS a few years ago. I had the great privilege to introduce him to Jesus before he died. The first thing that ALS attacked was his vocal cords; he could not talk in a way that you could understand him. We communicated completely via Instant Messenger. Whenever we ended our conversation he would say,—"Cath,—walk like Enoch—walk with God."

Dear friend, it is the one thing I believe that God desires for all of us—to walk with Him! Cloudland was a special place for me to see that it is possible to reach for the stars and go for it all! God is there in the valley, yet He is there on the mountain. He waits for us by the streams and helps us to be washed in the rivers. Every flower that blooms is our God saying "I love you"—and every bird we hear sing is proof that He is indeed right there—as close as the whisper of His name. Every butterfly we see tells us that He will take us from being worms and create us into beautiful butterflies if we will let Him. He promises to make ALL things beautiful in His special timing! Our part in this, is believing Him and taking Him at His Word!

Do I have it made and is life a jewel—heavens NO!!!! I still walk through valleys and then those beautiful mountaintop views! I enjoy and rest in the mountaintop—but in those valleys I listen and glean as much as I can all with one thing in mind! To know Him more! When life is over and it is time for me to go—I must remember that I take nothing with me except what I have done for Him. That includes resting, waiting and trusting in Him alone! It also includes the day to day stuff—you know, loving your neighbor as yourself, serving others and looking at the needs of our fellow man instead of ourselves. As my dear brother Solomon says: The conclusions when all has been said are fear God and keep His commandments! The fear of God is the beginning of wisdom—reverence Him and love Him with all your heart, all your soul and all your might! He is God and we are not—and in the knowledge of that amazingly He loves us so much that He gave us the greatest gift—Jesus His Son!

Roan Mountain Revisited

Chapter 12

Highlights: Trip back in time—
Hazards: Facing how far God brings us in spite of
          us

> *Yet this I call to mind and therefore I have*
> *hope: Because of the Lord's great love we are*
> *not consumed, for his compassions never fail.*
> *There are new every morning; great is your*
> *faithfulness. I say to myself, "The LORD is*
> *my portion; therefore I will wait for him."*
> *(Lamentations 3:22-23)*

Ten years after our last visit to Roan Mountain,
the Lord saw fit to allow us to go there once
more. When we first entered the area, I was flooded
with memories and amazed how incredible it still
was. When we got to the camp ground, I was filled

with memories of good and bad events, most of them in my own mind. In the midst of all the selfishness, breaking and suffering, God was there and He had a plan. He was breaking what I thought should be in my life and molding and preparing what He desired for my life. The majority of my suffering was because I was trying to hold on to **my** dreams, **my** hopes, **my** visions—when God—yes that same God of mine that created everything—has His own plans for me. Imagine just how deeply He desired me to follow His plan for me. My beautiful Heavenly Father knew that His plan for me would be the best and would make me the happiest!

As I walked around the campground I was overwhelmed with the presence of our Holy Father and Jesus! Jesus came so that we would never be alone—I can promise you through all my trials, dealing with sin, dying to my dreams, heartaches, sickness, death of loved ones and times of loneness, despair, brokenness, betrayal—HE was there! Most of those times without my realizing it, He was carrying me! When I was weak, He was my strength: when I was sorrowful, He became my comfort! Each time He pulled me closer to Him and walked with me, I found out something more amazing about my King and Lord! With each new adventure I fell deeper in love with my Jesus!

I thought back on all the incredible times. Even as I went to the bathroom, I remembered the little girl coming in completely sorrowful over the fact that someone had stepped on a "lil liteing bug". My daughter and I were in the bathroom, and this little one came in unaware that we were there and started talking in the Tennessee drawl—just being in that bathroom brought a tremendous chuckle to my heart! I wondered where that little girl was now. Did she ever realize just how much joy she brought to us by being just who God made her to be?

Sitting by the same creek that brought me such comfort just ten years before overwhelmed me once again. Remembering just how much mercy, grace, patience and love our Lord poured down on this broken vessel like me. Never once did He beat me over the head or say, "What are you thinking?" Then I thought of how many times I lost my patience with those around me that I was placed there to love. Listening to the sound of the water of the creek just brought me the realization that God is completely in control. He knew all my imperfections and still called me to be His! I felt so small in His great expanse of the world and wondered as the Psalmist did, "*Who am I that you think of me, who am I that you care for me?*" Do you know who we are? We are HIS!!!

Pull up a rock and sit by His precious creek and drink in the presence of a loving Savior and King that is saying, "Come to Me all who are weary and burdened and I will give you rest! Take My yoke upon you and learn from Me, because I am gentle and humble in heart!" (Matthew 11:28 HCSB) We forget that so much because we are so prideful—HE is so gentle and humble, and all He desires is for us to come to Him, lay our burdens down and rest!

When we left the campground, we were on our way up to see all the incredible sights we thought we remembered. The sights and sounds left me speech-less! The mountains were ablaze in reds, yellows, oranges and greens! It was the season of fall—deep in the month of October! *The mountains appeared sun kissed by God Himself! It was like the voice of our Father was saying, "Come up child—yes come up and see My majesty! Come see just how great I am—and how very tiny you are! Yet Child of mine, at the same time realize that YOU are the object I choose to pour all my affection on. My creation was only designed to draw you closer to Me and that you would see that I am indeed in control and don't need your help—and how great I AM! Never had it entered my mind that people would love creation and worship it—on the contrary, it was designed so that you would seek me and love me more. My word says that creation itself declares that there is a God! It cries out in a Son kissed voice— "Seek your God and then you will know Love, Joy, Peace and Kindness Himself! Then you will have abundant live!* "Abundant life is not "things" it is God!

As we walked on top of the mountain and drank in the smell of the spruce trees and stood in awe of the beauty and majesty that we were seeing I began to cry tears of joy! Realize that the same God who created all of this wants and thirsts for an intimate relationship with YOU!! That is all you can give him! Have you ever loved someone that just would not let you in—so many of us do this to our God and Jesus on a daily basis! The heart of the Father cries out to you...., *"Come sit a while and rest! Drop all you cares here at my feet and I will handle them for you! How I long to drink in your presence and delight myself in you!*" Scripture tells us that if we delight ourselves in the Lord He will give us the desires of our heart (see Psalm 37:4)! Once you start delighting yourself in HIM—you will find that the only desire you have is for more of HIM!

Then another scripture says in Isaiah 64:5 (NIV) "Since ancient times no one has heard, no ear has perceived, no eye has seen any God besides you, who acts on behalf of those who wait for Him!"

As we were up on top of the mountains we could not help but notice the beauty and crispness in the air! Funny, but when we got to the top, we could breathe better, see clearer—it was like all of our senses were awakened there! We left the craziness of our hometown and went away to the mountains.

Since hurricanes Katrina and Rita, our homeland has tripled in size, the highways are insane and that is putting it mildly, people are on edge and everything is booming—especially the prices. We were beginning to be consumed—with the cares of this world and it was hard to sit back and rest in our Lord—but once we got here we remembered God is in control— He can do everything so much better than we could ever imagine! Sin and the cares of this world have a way of shrinking God down to our size and exalting ourselves and our problems. Sometimes we must get away and remember—remember that above all, God IS in control! That is the Sabbath Day rest! It is all about remembering who He is and how little the world and our issues are!

As we walked in the clear blue sky the breeze was blowing and everything was so crisp! The smells were intoxicating and the sights beyond belief—up there on that mountain all the cares of the world seemed to disappear! It was then I realized that this is what the Scripture means that says: "Those who wait on the LORD shall renew their strength; they shall mount up with wings like eagles,—they shall run and not be weary, they shall walk and not faint" (Isaiah 40:31)! An eagle flies so high—high above all the junk on the ground—Ask yourself next time you are beginning to be really frazzled—"How high am I flying?" Dear friend, let us soar on the wings of Love Himself—let us rest and not grow weary, because if our Lord is for us, who can be against us? Even the worst situation will turn out for our good and His glory if we just keep our eyes fixed on Him and wait!

No picture would be able to show just how incredible the actual sight on top of Roan Mountain is! The same God that made all this beautiful creation, made you! The reason He made all of this was so you could see just how great is our God and HE LOVES YOU!!!

Grotto Falls

Chapter 13

Highlights: Beautiful Waterfalls
Hazards: Steep incline—strenuous hike

> *For I am the Lord, your God, who takes hold*
> *of your right hand and says to you, Do not*
> *fear; I will help you. (Isaiah 41:13)*

Grotto Falls hiking trail is right off Roaring Fork Road, the same road that Rainbow falls is on. The only thing I can remember about Grotto Falls is both times we hiked it, we went up and down the mountain very fast! Each time we approached Grotto Falls, a storm was brewing, and then it exploded on us right when we reached the top. The crazy thing about storms is we never stop to see the beauty of what is around us and continue to be thankful in the midst of the storm.

The first time we attempted Grotto Falls my husband, children and I were excited and ready for the hike! It was only a 2.4-mile hike. Compared with Chimney Tops, which was a four mile hike straight up and down. Grotto seemed like a piece of cake! Really the hike is not that bad, although it is labeled in the books as strenuous. The first time we went up, the weather seemed to change suddenly. We had been exploring the old buildings on Roaring Fork Road and everything was beautiful! The sun was shining, a breeze was blowing gently an occasional cloud floated past and blocked the sun, but none of us were aware that right down the road, a storm was brewing! In the midst of the mountains and trees, storm clouds can be hidden when you are at the base of the mountain! On the hike up the mountain, we began to notice that the air was becoming very still. It was becoming hard to breathe because of the stifling heat and because there was no breeze, not even a hint of one. As we hiked up the mountain, we thought that the mountain itself was shielding us from the breeze because we were going round and round instead of side to side. All of us were becoming really tired and we had to rest quite frequently because of the lack of fresh air!

I thought how many times in life we just wander through then suddenly—there it is! We notice the air is thinning and wonder what is going on? Everything seems to be OK, but there is just something…you know what I mean. You can't put your finger on it, but you can sense something is just not right!

All the way up the mountain that is exactly what we felt like. The 1.2 miles to the top seemed like forever! It was stifling hot, the air was so thick it was hard to get a deep breath, and no matter how much we sat and rested it did no good because it was so hot! We kept looking up to see if we could notice any storm clouds, but the trees blocked the view of the sky. All we could see were trees. Down in the city people could see the storm clouds brewing—but there we were—surrounded by the trees and too close to tell. Have you ever felt in your heart,—*"What in the world is going on?"*

Maybe you were so close to the forests all you could see is trees, instead of seeing the forest! Well, there we were—so close to the trees that trees were all we could see! So many times in our lives, that is exactly how we feel, like walking in a dark dream with stifling air and no breeze! It is during those times that we must just walk in faith!

I can see Jesus walking up to the hill of Golgotha carrying the cross, with the only thing in His face was the screaming people crying, "Crucify Him!" and the tremendous pain He was enduring! I am sure the air was stifling and hot and His body racked with pain—yet He knew He was getting ready to endure some of the most horrid pain yet! Nailed to a cross and then having all the people He was dying for rejecting Him and taunting Him. Jesus was Holiness Himself—given to us to walk through the deepest darkness ever so that when we walk through those times; He could be an effective intercessor for us! There is nothing that we walk through that Jesus does not only understand but He also has a plan in the midst of it!

Finally we reached the top of Grotto Falls, and the only thing I remembered the first time was taking off my hiking boots and putting my feet in the cold water of the river to refresh me. I had never been so overheated and worn out in a hike in my life! The cold water of the river felt good—yet I never remembered the falls and their beauty! I was overwhelmed with the heat, stillness of the air and my own exhaustion caused by the atmosphere around us! Not once did I even realize that a storm was brewing right on top of that mountain! The trees were so thick we could not see the sky. In our society today, everyone wants to just pop a pill and make it all feel better and make it all go away! No one wants to fight through the battles, storms, fire and the waters—just give me a pill to make the pain go away! It can be emotional pain, physical pain, relationship pain—whatever it is, as a Christian you must walk through it! You have to always remember there is a plan—it may be unseen, but God is not surprised by the trial, tribulation and suffering you may be going through! Also, ALWAYS remember that it does come to pass—never to stay!

Suddenly it started thundering! My husband is deathly afraid of lightening. When he was a child, he was in a lightning storm and lightning struck just a few feet from him and scared him to death! He still runs from this fear instead of facing it and realizing that God is well able to protect him in the midst of the storms! This is the man that has one speed—slow. We were always way ahead of him and would have to stop and wait for him. Suddenly he took off headed down the mountain, and before we had our shoes on he was gone! The fear had overtaken him and was driving him on! Fear causes you to continually run, run, run! I see so many people running today! They have forgotten the gift of stopping and smelling the roses, and because of the wounds inside of them, they run! Instead of stopping and allowing God to deliver them by allowing them to fight through it— they run! They run to pills, hobbies, work, busyness, TV, computers, movies—you name it and they are running!

It seemed like our trip up that mountain took forever—yet before we knew it, we had already made the 1.2-mile trip down and were headed for our car! Years later I did not remember the trip up the mountain or the short stay on top or the trip down. The only thing I remembered was the intense staleness of the air and the stagnant heat. Fear, fatigue, discomfort, pain and pressure have a tendency to rob us of the enjoyment of wonderful things in our lives. That trip I am sure was beautiful—but I could never tell you because not only was I dealing with the heat exhaustion, the stagnant air and muscle aches, but I was also dealing with the complaints and fears of those with me too! I realized that storms have a great tendency to stir up the things that we really don't really want to deal with. But regardless how we felt, the storm stirred all these hindrances up and there they were for all to see!

The sad thing is that every one of us just climbed in the car, got something to drink and went on our merry way! Did any of us deal with the fears, pain, heartache, pressures that it stirred up—No! I can see that years later—some of our family members are still holding on to the same fears that have stopped us from moving forward with our Lord! These are like hooks attached on our body! Every time we start to go forward—, **Bam!**— the enemy just takes a hook and stops us dead in our tracks and we don't know what hit us or what's going on!

Just this year we went back to Grotto Falls again. When we got to the trailhead it was already late and guess what? A storm was brewing—but we knew it was brewing! In spite of our better judgment because we knew that we would be going home in a couple of days, we decided to go ahead and hit the trail! This time, the wind blew wildly on one side of the mountain—the other side the air was again stagnant! Darkness was closing in so we knew that we would have to seriously move fast to get to the top and back before it became dark and the road would possibly be closed and we would be stuck on that Roaring Fork zigzagging road for the night!!

I did not have the trail book with me therefore I did not realize that Grotto was a strenuous hike. We met several people coming down leisurely from the top of the mountain. All of them told us that the falls were wonderful and beautiful and well worth seeing! I did not even remember the falls from the first trip! That encouraging word spurred us on! I have never moved so fast, and I was surprised at how fast I was moving especially after two major surgeries that year and many months of recovery! You could feel the dampness in the air, the warning of hard rain to come! Indeed a storm was brewing! This time I was almost prepared. I had my poncho and umbrella, but I had teeny shoes on. I decided to do the hike with my teeny shoes instead of putting on my hiking boots! I was trying to hurry up and forgot some very important equipment! Those boots protected my feet from rock and slipping. Right when we got to the top the rain started! I got a very short glimpse of the falls before we had to start heading down. I didn't even remember these beautiful falls from the first trip, they went on for yards! The wonderful sound of the falls was such a powerful sympathy, and I could not even remember them from before! How? I realized that the storms in our lives rob us of the very beauty that is right in front of our eyes to see! In the midst—GOD is there! In the midst of the storm—He is there!

We forget that He never leaves us nor forsakes us! We stopped long enough for me to take a quick picture of the falls—and not a good one at that—and began the hike down the mountain! We stayed on the top for approximately three minutes! We were running! We had to hurry—the storm was coming—run, run, run! That was the only thing in my mind! The hike down that mountain was dangerous to say the least! It began to rain—then the wind picked up. I grabbed my poncho and put it on with great difficulty because of the wind. The camera was secured under my poncho and I grabbed the hood and started hiking as fast as my feet could carry me down the mountain! I had to hold onto the hood of the poncho for it to protect me from the rain! The rocks became very slippery and several times because I had teeny shoes on, I almost slipped and fell! The drop-off on the side was very long and steep so I stayed as close to the mountain wall as I could! The darkness was beginning to get thicker then with the rain and trees it was becoming increasingly hard to see the next footing! The steepness of the mountain caused me several times to run down and with the camera equipment, coat and fear steadily driving me on. I began to feel panicked! I had to stop and tell myself that God was still in control and that I was going to be OK!!! Sometimes we just need to give ourselves a good talk! I was afraid that the road would close because it was getting very dark! Many of those winding roads closed at dark because the steepness of the cliff on the sides of the road. Was this one of them?

The rain was beginning to pound down on us, and the bottom of my pants and feet were now soaked! Amazingly, the poncho was keeping me dry despite the fight to hold the hood in place—then I noticed my husband coming down holding the umbrella in his hand! I asked him if he was going to use that thing or not? As he shook his head no, I grabbed it and opened it up! At least now I could see because the umbrella was shielding the rain from my eyes!

Well, we made it down to the fork finally! There was the parking lot and the car—and behold—I saw another car going—my fears of the road closure were destroyed! We were now safe—when we got into the car—we both looked at each other and laughed! My husband was soaked from head to toe—he had the proper protection in his hand but refused to use it! I was soaked from knees down—but at least the top portion of me was dry! The equipment available to me was indeed used, and because of that I came out much better than he did!

In our storms God has given us His word, His armor, His songs of praise, His presence and prayer—but how many of us use them in storms or do we just let them sit by and run on our own! We will come out—but how we are affected by them and the outcome of victory will be determined by how many of God's tools we choose to use! In Isaiah 43:2 (NIV) He tells us plainly:

> When you pass through the waters, I will be with you; and when you pass through the rivers, they will not sweep over you. When you walk through the fire, you will not be burned; the flames will not set you ablaze. (Isaiah 43:2 NIV, emphasis added.)

These storms will come—but how we handle our storms will determine our outcome and if we will have to go through them again or if we pass the test!

Prayerfully, I will be able to go up Grotto Falls again! This time I am going to check the weather forecast and bring all the proper equipment, and I know that the next time we climb this mountain, I want to be prepared! I am sure that there were so many beauties that I missed because I was driven by the storm, fears, logic and just being me. I don't want to miss anything God has for me—on whatever mountain top, or valley, or hill God has for me to climb! Grotto Falls taught me to learn to relax in the storm, trust in Him and enjoy!

The Drought

Chapter 14

There is a river whose streams make glad the city of God, the holy place where the Most High dwells. (Psalm 46:4)

We were given the great opportunity of returning to Tennessee to visit some of the wonderful places we remembered. Tennessee had been in a drought. Their normal rainfall was around 60 inches a year and what they had received was only 20 inches for the year. We were there in October, so imagine just how badly they were in need of rain. My beautiful creeks were almost dried up and many places the water was stagnant. Without the flow of the water fish were beginning to die and the creeks could not flow like they had. There was no longer the sound of the creeks as we drove along the roads and even in the hikes we had to stop and listen hard to hear any movement at all. Everywhere we went it was like this. The drought had taken more than just lack of water away; it was also taking the whole environment and affecting it in a negative way! The sights were still beautiful but lacked the whole affect that it had on us, because there was little water.

It was almost heartbreaking to see these once full flowing rivers that seemed to sing as they flowed along, become almost still! As I walked along the rivers, I realized that this is indeed just how a Christian can become. When we do not sit and allow the flow of the Holy Spirit of our Lord to pour down upon us we are walking around trying to reach the world when we are in need of a touch from God! The reason the drought was there was because of the lack of rainfall. The reason we become dry is because of our lack of sitting in the rainfall that can only come from reading our Bibles, praying and just plain sitting in His beautiful presence! We wonder where the excitement of becoming a child of the King has gone, and we wonder why we just do not have enough to give out and we wonder why we aren't effective anymore!

As I thought about it, I realized that everything was affected by this drought. At first the river still flowed somewhat, and in many places we went there was still a trickle—but nothing like we knew could exist! It was so sad! I noticed that there were not many deer or any of the other animals that we had seen in the past. Where had they gone, they went where there was water. Then the trees were not as full as they had been, because the river was not able to water them like it had when it was full and flowing. And last was the fish—even they were being affected by the stagnant water. Because there was no flow, the water lacked the air they needed to breathe. Even the river did not seem as happy and alive as it had been in the past! Actually it was quite sad to sit there knowing the possibility that could be there and to see what was there now.

You see, the river is at the mercy of our God for its refills. There is nothing it can do to make rain—it is totally dependent on God. But we are able to go and choose to sit at the river of God and drink in His wonderful presence. When we do not choose to do so, many people and places are affected. You see my friend, no one is an island. We are placed here for a purpose and a reason. What we do or don't do affects many—we may not understand it fully until we do get to eternity, but I can tell you we will be held responsible for it.

There is a beautiful praise song that the chorus says:

Let the river flow, let His river flow,
Holy Spirit come and move in power—
Let the river flow—let the river flow!

You see, it is entirely up to us to let His river flow through us onto a lost and dying world. Every person counts and matters to God Almighty. His word says in John 3:16 that God so loved the world that He gave His only begotten Son that whoever would believe in Him would not perish and find everlasting life. Jesus gave it all—He laid down His life for us all to live and all He asks in return is to allow His river of living water to flow through us so all may know that He is there waiting with open arms of love for who so ever will come. We are His ambassadors, as the scripture says, like He is pleading through us. If we allow the water to stop in our own lives, then who are we kidding? It will affect others too.

A couple of days before we left, it rained that night and the next day a very slow but steady rain. It did not seem like it was much rain, but amazingly just that little bit made a big difference in all the creeks. You see, it flows down-hill. You water someone, and then they water someone else, and so on and so on. It is the same with the creeks—, one creek flows down into another, and it ends up affecting every stream of water all the way down the mountain! It was wonderful to see the creeks flowing once again, and you know what? The animals began to return, and the fly fishermen began to fish again, and everything began to return to normal.

Dearest friend, how is your river flowing right now? Is it stagnant or is it flowing down? For our rivers, sin is the thing that can stop them. The Word says, "If we confess our sins and He is faithful and just to forgive us our sins and to cleanse us from all unrighteousness." (1John 1:9 NKJV) Do not hold on to anything that is not of God. It is not worth it. Remember, it is not just about you—you are no island—there are many watching you and many who count on you to have that word in season. Trust in God and just come to Him openly and plainly. He will by no means turn you out. People may reject you, but if you come before our Lord with a humble heart—I know for a fact that He will cleanse you, turn you around, place you back on your feet, and say in such an incredible loving voice, "Try again dear child, I know you can do it!"

We serve a very loving and gracious Father, not one waiting to beat you on the head because you goofed up! Run to Him, let Him embrace you, wipe away your tears, and set you once more on the Rock Christ Jesus! Remember this, every tear you shed He saves in a bottle, and when the time is right, He will make every tear or sorrow become a tear of joy!

Let your river flow, dear friend—and let all see your good works so that they may glorify your Father in Heaven (see Matthew 5:16).

In Conclusion

Chapter 15

And we know that in all things God works for the good of those who love him, who have been called according to his purpose. For those God foreknew he also predestined to be conformed to the likeness of his Son, that he might be the firstborn among many brothers.
(Romans 8:28-29)

If I began to explain all the trials, sufferings, losses, physical suffering, blessings, understanding and knowledge that I went through in this past year, you would be as astonished as I am. But I can testify how the Lord our God not only walked with me through each storm, river and fire, but many times He picked me up and carried me through! In every new challenge I learned something more profound than ever before about the Love of my life—my Heavenly Father, the

Lord Jesus Christ and the Holy Spirit! Dear friend I tell you that you are never alone — He is there — when you are so weak that you do not think you can take one more step, He will pick you up and carry you if you let Him, and He will make you strong! Only then will you begin to know how strong yet very tender His everlasting arms are! How deep and wide, long and high is His great love for you and your fellow man, how there is nothing impossible with Him and nothing that will separate you from His great love for you! He is well able to take the most horrible looking situation and turn it around to become the most wonderful thing that could have ever happened to you!

He is GOD and we are not! He alone is the Potter and we are His clay! The most important thing to understand about our Lord is the fact that this holy, incredible and wonderful Creator of the whole universe is deeply and unbelievably in love with YOU!!! His greatest desire is for you to KNOW Him and that you would allow Him to know you in an intimate way! The only way for this to happen is that you go through "stuff" so He can show you Himself and who He desires to be in your life! The poem "Footprints" has a whole new meaning for me now. I felt myself being physically carried by our Lord so many times through this past year — even when people were leaning on me for strength, they had no idea that I was not leaning, but being carried by Him. Because I allowed Him to carry me, little did they know that He was carrying them too!

Psalm 46:10 says, "Be still, and KNOW that I AM God!" (Emphasis added.) That is the key, dear friend—there are times we just have to say like 2 Chronicles 20 (emphasis added). "We have no power over this vast army that is attacking us, but our eyes are upon YOU!" In these moments we are to get our eyes off how weary we are in well doing, how weak we are, how hard the circumstances are, how much pain we are in or that our loved ones are in and focus on God, our Heavenly Father, that created the universe—everything we see and can't even begin to see—and just know that He is God and we are not! Then praise Him—for even the hurting things and for every circumstance because it is ALL working for your good and His glory!

Yes, 2007 was a very hard year—yet at the same time, it was an incredible year! There is no other year that I can say that I learned more about my Lord and if I had to do it again to get what I have gotten from Him, I would! HE is worth it all! Bitter/sweet! That is how I describe this year! There was so much bitter—yet with the cross of Jesus He made it all so sweet!

He is standing there at the door of your heart asking if you will let Me in.—Are you tired, are you weary of well doing, are you so emotionally drained that you cannot understand how you can put one foot in front of the other? I have been there, my friend. There is only one answer I have for you:—Be still and know that He is God!

Remember, unless a seed falls to the ground and dies, it cannot spring up and produce fruit. Let it all go—and give that seed to the One who created seeds. He will plant it and then one day down the road He will come with a bushel basket full of fruit! You will ask, "Lord, where did this come from, who bore me these—I was bereaved and barren—". He will show you that those who WAIT upon the Lord shall indeed renew their strength and they will mount up with wings of eagles. You who wait on the Lord will not be disappointed.

It takes time for fruit to be produced—wait on Him, and in the process of waiting get to know Him like you never dreamed you could. He is there waiting for you to call on His name. He is there—open your heart and see! You haven't been waiting for Him—actually He has been waiting for you to trust in Him!

Yes 2007 was a bitter sweet year, but I know when this year is all said and done, I will always look back and remember the end of that year when my Lord God took all the lemons of that year and made the sweetest lemonade! I can see us sitting down together drinking that sweetened lemonade reminiscing over the incredible things that He accomplished in and through me. What a time that will be—I know we will laugh and cry a bit—yet I do know that ALL of it worked not only for my good but also that others will see Him in the midst of the trials and then glorify my Heavenly Father for all He has done! Wow—what a year it has been!

Dear Friend,

My prayer is that these little stories become a call from your Heavenly Father for you to come and sit with Him and glean from Him. HE would love to take you in His arms and surround you with His loving-kindness and tender mercies. I pray that you would fall in love with my Lord more deeply than I have and that you would run into His presence to hear the loving words that He desires to speak to you. I would love to hear from you—you can write me at cath1224@charter.net. As you have read this serious of stories from the Lord, may your eyes be opened to see His face and that your ears be opened to hear His voice and that your heart would accept what He would speak to you. Words alone could never tell you just how much He loves you—so just look to the cross. He paid the ultimate sacrifice. He gave it all on the cross. If you do not know the Lord Jesus as your Savior, all it takes is a simple prayer from your heart. Just say this little prayer:

Dearest Lord Jesus—I need your help; you see, I am a sinner who has sinned against you and one who is in need of a Savior. I invite you to come into my heart and become my Lord and Savior. Jesus take over my life and make all the weak spots new—help me to walk in a manner that would please you and show me where I need to go to learn more about You. My prayer, Lord, is that I would see Your face and hear Your beautiful voice—therefore, hide me in the cleft of the rock as You pass by! I thank You for saving me, coming to me, wiping my rap sheet clean and for healing me. Thank you, Lord, in Jesus Name.

For those of you who have been wounded by life, there is hope. He came to set the captive free. Dear one, freedom is yours—all you have to do is take it and receive it!

Read His love letters to you that are in His book, the Bible—let Him speak to you and whisper in your ear—"Come to me all who are weary and heavy laden and I will give you rest for your souls (Matthew 11:28)! He loves you, dear friend—now just bask in His goodness!

Blessings in Christ,

CPSIA information can be obtained at www.ICGtesting.com
Printed in the USA

243499LV00001B/1/P